The Irish Celtic
Magical Tradition

The Irish Celtic Magical Tradition

Steve Blamires

Aquarian/Thorsons
An Imprint of HarperCollinsPublishers

The Aquarian Press
An Imprint of HarperCollins*Publishers*
77-85 Fulham Palace Road,
Hammersmith, London W6 8JB

Published by The Aquarian Press 1992
1 3 5 7 9 10 8 6 4 2

© Steve Blamires 1992

Steve Blamires asserts the moral right to
be identified as the author of this work

A catalogue record for this book
is available from the British Library

ISBN 1 85538 149 4

Typeset by Harper Phototypesetters Limited,
Northampton, England
Printed in Great Britain by
Mackays of Chatham, Kent

To Sue
for making it all worthwhile

Contents

Acknowledgements

I wish to express my sincere thanks to the Irish Texts Society, and in particular to Dr Elizabeth A. Gray, for allowing me to quote so extensively from her translation of *Cath Maige Tuired*. I also wish to thank Courtney Davis for supplying the beautiful artwork which illustrates this text, and, most important of all, the host of known and unknown Bards and story-tellers who had the foresight and the good sense to remember things long after they would otherwise have been forgotten.

Introduction:
The Legend of
The Battle of Moytura

It is often assumed by those starting on a magical or spiritual quest that only Eastern and Oriental religions and philosophies provide accurate teachings and instructions concerning the correct way of living in harmony with oneself and one's environment. It is also commonly assumed that there is not, and never has been, a complementary Western or native system. This, however, is definitely not the case. It will be demonstrated in this book that there is an equally valid and viable Western tradition that meets and satisfies the physical, mental and spiritual needs of its practitioners as fully as does any Oriental system. Sufficient information and guidance will be given throughout this book which will enable the reader on completion to progress to whatever level he or she desires, either alone or as a member of a group practising this native tradition.

The main stumbling block for searchers after such a Western tradition is usually the assumption that there are no ancient magical books, no recognized definitive written works detailing, either specifically or by way of parable, a philosophy, religion or magical system which can be studied and tested. Because of this apparent gap it is often incorrectly assumed by students of the occult that either there never was such a structured form of guidance and teaching or, if there was, it has been lost in the mists of time and is no longer obtainable.

Fortunately this is not the case, and there is indeed a wealth of written material still available today which is

equal in its spiritual content to the well-known works of
the East such as the *Upanishads*, the *Tao Te Ching*, the
Bhagavad Gita, the Egyptian *Book of the Dead* and the
plethora of other such works very much in vogue among
today's students of things spiritual and magical. The
difference is that whereas most Eastern philosophies are
nowadays easily accessible – mainly as a result of the
wealth of books written about them which explain their
more subtle points – their Western equivalents are
couched in the form of stories and legends which, on the
surface, appear to be no more than barbaric and fantastic
accounts of rather brutal battles and the goings-on of
extremely dubious characters. Consequently such works
have been largely ignored by those on magical or spiritual
quests, and it is very difficult to obtain any form of
instruction or interpretation concerning these legends,
either in written or oral form. This situation has been
changing in recent years, however. There has been an
upsurge of interest in the Arthuriad, the Welsh Mabinogi
legends and the Matter of Britain generally. The term
'Western Mystery Tradition' has been coined to cover these
areas of native research and study, and readers unfamiliar
with this body of learning are advised to study the books
listed in the Bibliography, as many of these recommended
works have been written by authors who have not only
deeply studied the Western Mystery Tradition but are also
active practitioners of it.

There is, however, another even more ancient and
powerful system still extant in the West; details of it are
to be found in the surviving legends of the Irish Celts,
legends which have been preserved in ancient
manuscripts and, to a certain extent, in the living oral
tradition of Ireland and the West of Scotland. Several such
Irish Celtic legends contain within them the seeds of the
whole Celtic philosophy in general, and each individual
legend demonstrates specific points and aspects of this
Irish tradition in detail.

This book will concentrate on an examination of the
ancient Irish legend of *The Battle of Moytura*. This legend,
as will be shown, contains within it the essence of the
Irish Celtic spiritual and magical system as well as a great
deal of practical instruction and information on the

various techniques and attitudes needed to live successfully both in this world and in the Otherworld.

In order to understand and appreciate fully the contents of this ancient Irish allegory it is necessary to put aside temporarily one's modern way of thinking and outlook on life and to adopt, as far as possible, the same way of thinking and understanding as was used by the ancient Irish Celts, who put this unique system together originally over two thousand years ago.

To do this, two main changes in attitude have to be adopted which will help to open up a deeper understanding of the incredible contents of this seemingly simple tale of battles and magical feats.

The first major change necessary is to do away with one's normal concept of linear time, the neat and orderly flow of events, one after the other, in a straightforward and to a certain extent predictable manner. The events described in *The Battle of Moytura* seem to the modern mind to jump forwards and backwards in time and, in some places, to be outside the effect of time altogether. This does not matter. Simply accept such passages as they are and do not try to fit them into our modern concept of time which dictates that everything must follow the neat order of Start - Middle - End. As will be demonstrated, our modern concept of linear time is very inaccurate; once this is understood and accepted a great deal of apparently puzzling or meaningless information becomes very clear and valuable.

The second change in thinking, and probably the most important, is to look upon everything, absolutely everything, as existing on three distinct yet interlocking levels. These levels, for ease of reference, we will call the *physical level*, the *mental level*, and the *spiritual level*. This tripartite outlook on life is crucial to a true understanding of the Celtic philosophy and magical system, and if the reader can adopt this attitude initially without questioning it, then it will soon become obvious to him or her why it is necessary, and why it is in fact the most accurate way to view this world, the Otherworld, and all that both contain. The truth behind this will become apparent as the inner meanings of the text are explained.

Fuller explanations of both of these concepts, non-linear

time and the three levels, will be given as and when appropriate during our examination of the text of the legend.

Practical Work

It is sometimes asked what is the relevance of such an ancient Irish Celtic philosophy, which is based on thinking thousands of years old, to humanity today? The same question could of course be asked of any of the world's main religions, all of which are hundreds if not thousands of years old. The answer to this will become obvious as we examine the legend of *The Battle of Moytura* and discover that it deals in microcosm and macrocosm with concepts that are beyond time and are therefore just as relevant today as they were at any other stage of humanity's progression. This will also help to demonstrate what was said above about the need to change our normal understanding of time.

Each chapter of the book will end with a section entitled *Practical Work*, which, when combined with the text just read, will start to help the reader to understand this intricate and fulfilling system for him- or herself. It should be stressed here that this book and the practical techniques it describes are of an introductory nature only, and should not be seen as being the entire Irish Celtic magical system in condensed form. There are many books available giving very detailed instruction and guidance on magic generally, and one or two dealing with Celtic magic specifically, but unfortunately most of these books assume the reader to have at least some knowledge if not personal practice and experience of magical and Inner Workings.

This book, however, starts with the assumption that the reader is entirely new to the subject, and from this basis steadily builds up to a point where, by the end of the book and having completed all the Practical Work, the reader will then be able to carry on with his or her progress by consulting some of the more 'advanced' books listed in the Bibliography. I would stress that practitioners of any of the other many magical systems in use today, even ones which claim to be Celtic, should likewise start this book on the assumption that they are entirely new to magic generally. As will be revealed, there are many subtle differences between this system and most of the others, and to adopt the attitude, 'Oh, yes, I know all about this,' could lead to misunderstandings and difficulties later on.

For those new to the Inner Workings described in the Practical Work, which can be classed under the generic term of *Pathworking* (sometimes also called *Guided Meditation*), which is so popular today, there are a couple of important points to bear in mind if you are to make any real progress in this Work:

1. It must be remembered that what you are seeing, hearing and doing during these Inner Workings is absolutely real, and should therefore be treated as such.
2. Any person whom you should encounter during such an Inner Working is likewise very real, and must be treated with the same respect, courtesy and general good manners as you would display when making a new acquaintance in this world.
3. Because of the effect these Inner Workings will start to have on your Inner Self, it is not advisable to attempt the Practical Work if you are suffering from any form of physical or mental illness, even if such illness is being medically treated. Likewise, it is not advisable to attempt the Practical Work while under the influence of drugs or alcohol, and it is best not to have eaten for some two or three hours before beginning.
4. It is not necessary, or indeed advisable, to adopt any Yoga-style postures while undertaking an Inner Working. The best position is simply to sit upright in a high-backed chair with your feet together on the ground and your hands resting gently in your lap. Your eyes can be open or closed depending on your personal preference, but wherever and whenever you perform the Practical Work it is advisable to ensure that you will not be disturbed by such things as people entering the room or a phone ringing.
5. It is good practice to note down in a diary kept specifically for this purpose any realizations, sensations, feelings, encounters, etc. you had during the

Inner Working. Once any such notes have been made a hot drink and light snack is advisable, to help completely close down the Inner parts that have been stimulated by the Inner Working.

If these simple guidelines are observed, and if the Practical Work is followed through in the order given in this book, then the reader should be sufficiently able by the time he or she has finished this book to carry on with further studies, to whatever level he or she feels comfortable with, either through his or her own abilities, by studying more advanced books, or by contacting one of the better magical groups offering safe and graded training.

One final point regarding the Practical Work - it should be remembered that the Irish Celts lived very close to Nature, to the Green World, and considered themselves to be subject to exactly the same laws of the Green World as were the animals and plants around them. It was for this reason that they made themselves so familiar with the ways and workings of the Green World. It is therefore extremely important for practitioners of this system today to likewise make themselves aware of the goings-on in the Green World around them. For those who live in rural settings this should be fairly easy, but for those who live in the towns and cities there is absolutely no substitute for making the effort to visit the countryside, or seaside, as often as possible - and in as many seasons and weather conditions as possible, not just on nice, sunny summer days! This in itself is a very important part of the Practical Work, and should be enjoyed as such.

The Book Itself

The full title of *The Battle of Moytura* in the original Irish is *Cath Maige Turedh An Scel-sa Sis & Genemain Bres Meic Elathan & A Righe* which translates as *This Tale Below is the Battle of Maige Tuired and the Birth of Bres Son of Elatha and His Reign*. Note the triple aspect of this full title: a battle, a birth, and a king's reign. There are only two complete original manuscript copies extant today. The older is from the first half of the sixteenth century and was committed to writing by the scribe Gilla

Riabhach O'Cleirigh, Son of Tuathal, Son of Tadhg Cam O'Cleirigh, and is in the Old Irish language. The second manuscript was written between 1651 and 1652 by David Duigenan, and is in Middle Irish. Both, however, are believed to have come from a text which was known in the ninth century, and which in turn was based on oral traditions of immeasurable antiquity. Its very longevity speaks volumes.

Because these old Celtic Pagan legends were written down many centuries after their original oral telling, and because the people who wrote them down were Christian monks, it is often taken as fact that the versions we have inherited today must be corrupted or altered, perhaps even deliberately, and therefore probably bear little resemblance to their original form. On the surface this argument appears plausible and quite likely but, on closer thought and examination, it soon becomes apparent that it is an error to assume this automatically.

It has often been argued that the original oral tellings must have gradually changed and been altered and embellished by each individual story-teller over the many long years these tales were told, the result being that it is no longer possible today to say that any one version is the true and original one. This, however, assumes that the original story-tellers were incapable of remembering the full story verbatim as they had heard it, or that they wilfully changed the content of the tale for reasons of their own.

It is highly unlikely that either of these suppositions are correct. The main fault with this argument is that it is based on our modern inability to remember long spoken passages, and, secondly, upon our equally modern desire to express ourselves in our own, individual way. These assumptions do not take into account the way the ancient Celts - who after all were the ones telling the story in the first place - regarded the importance of memory; nor do they take into account the need that existed to pass on spoken words accurately and precisely.

With the invention of writing neither a retentive memory nor the ability to recall long oral pieces verbatim was so important, and gradually over the centuries we have lost the memory capacity which our forebears most definitely had. Indeed, the Celts were wise enough to see both the dangers and advantages of this new form of communication known as writing, and in order to preserve the memory abilities of their holy men, the Druids, they forbade them writing down any of their secular works. There was no such prohibition on the layman, however, as it was recognized that writing did have distinct advantages in the commercial world.

It is feasible then that the legends which eventually came to be written down in the seventh-to-ninth centuries were accurate copies of the extant oral tradition. This is also borne out by the fact that for several centuries the two traditions existed side by side. The ordinary Celt did not have the luxury of books nor the ability to read and therefore still depended entirely upon the spoken word. The monks on the other hand, who wrote these spoken words down, would also have been familiar with the oral tradition, and it would have been pointless for them to set down in writing (for writing was a very laborious and expensive business), works which they knew to be inaccurate or simply wrong.

It is also often argued that the written legends are not faithful reproductions of the oral legends because the Christian scribes edited or changed the very Pagan nature of the legends and deliberately altered them in an attempt to convert the common people to the new Christian religion. This again is highly unlikely for several reasons.

It must be remembered that the Christian monks had originally been Pagan Celts, and these tales, as will be demonstrated in this book, were not just stories or fanciful fairy-tales but the very basis on which the whole of their society was constructed (on three levels, remember), and it would have been unthinkable, even on the part of converts to the new Christian religion, deliberately to alter or otherwise tamper with such important information. This fact can be seen by the way the Irish Catholic church incorporated a very great deal of the existing Pagan religious beliefs and practices into its own teachings, much to the annoyance and eventual fury of Rome.

In the case of this particular legend there is no evidence whatsoever of the text having been altered by over-zealous scribes, and although there are a couple of places where the Christian scribe did insert a few comments of his own, these do not in any way alter the sense of the story nor attempt to discredit the events being described. It will also be seen that the text contains some very explicit sexual descriptions as well as references to some very basic bodily functions, normally not talked about even today. It seems very unlikely then that if the monks' aim was to edit and change the old Pagan legends into acceptable Christian versions they would have left in such un-Christian passages.

The important point about any of these ancient Celtic legends is that the information they contain goes beyond such things, and 'speaks' directly to the innermost part of the reader, who instinctively knows it is correct. They are truly timeless and, as will be shown in the following pages, they adopt and adapt themselves to the times in which they are being read. Therefore their spiritual instruction and guidance is as valid now as it was a thousand years ago and will be a thousand years hence.

It is not my intention in this book to get involved in academic arguments such as whether the legend has been changed or not, whether the events described relate to a real battle or whether they are purely fictional, or whether the various races mentioned in the story actually existed and can be identified today. Many books have already dealt with these subjects; a few are mentioned in the Bibliography for the benefit of those readers who wish to investigate such points for themselves.

In order to give a comprehensive explanation and demonstration as to the wealth of symbolism and instruction contained within *The Battle of Moytura*, it has been necessary to split the text into smaller sections (167 in all), so that all of its main concepts and information can be extracted and digested before the next batch is processed. This may be a bit confusing to the reader, who may wish to follow the story from start to finish all at one go, but I would suggest that he or she read this book as it is laid out; it can then be re-read as a whole once the individual parts have been examined and understood.

I have tried as much as possible to split the narrative

into sections which are complete in themselves and which make sense if read in isolation apart from the rest of the main story. There are however some passages which are so archaic and obscure that it is impossible even to attempt a guess as to what they originally symbolized. This, however, does not matter. Most of the narrative can still be read and understood perfectly; the uninterpretable passages do not affect the overall outcome of our dissection of the symbolism contained within the rest of the legend.

These totally obscure passages in an ironic way do serve an important function, in that they demonstrate very clearly that the physical, mental and spiritual needs of humanity have altered as our understanding of the world around us has changed. When the legend was originally told these now obscure passages would have had an immediate relevance to the Celtic listener, and he or she would have been able to see and understand the symbolism and information which they contained. As our needs and understanding of life have altered through the centuries so the information contained within parts of the legend has lost its relevance and is of no use to us today. This is a perfectly natural function and simply reflects what happens in the Green World, the World of Nature – when something has lost its relevance or its ability to adopt to changing circumstances it is done away with or modified to suit the times. We call this evolution in the plant and animal world, and this same principle of evolution can be applied to the texts of the Celtic legends. Perhaps some of the major world religions would do well to pay heed to this important point, and to accept that parts of their teachings are outdated and need to be allowed to evolve. Evolution brings life, stagnation brings death.

Finally I would like to add that the translation I have chosen to use for these two old manuscripts is the version available through the Irish Texts Society (whose address is given in the Bibliography), as this is the most complete and thorough translation I could find. I have kept to the same section numbering employed by the Irish Texts Society, but it should be noted that the original manuscripts are not split into such neat sections. I have used the sections in this current examination simply to ease textual references and in order to split the text into easy-to-handle blocks.

Chapter 1
Sections 1 - 6

My examination of *The Battle of Moytura* begins with the first nine sections of the legend, which are probably the most important and contain within them the essence of the Celtic philosophical, religious and magical beliefs. In this chapter I will focus on the first six sections; Chapter 2 examines Sections 7 to 9 more fully.

1. The Tuatha De Danann were in the northern islands of the world, studying occult lore and sorcery, druidic arts, witchcraft and magical skills, until they surpassed the sages of the pagan arts.
2. They studied occult lore, secret knowledge and diabolic arts in four cities: Falias, Gorias, Murias and Findias.
3. From Falias was brought the Stone of Fal, which was located in Tara. It used to cry out beneath every king that would take Ireland.
4. From Gorias was brought the spear which Lug had. No battle was ever sustained against it, or against the man who held it in his hand.
5. From Findias was brought the sword of Nuadu. No one ever escaped from it once it was drawn from its deadly sheath, and no one could resist it.
6. From Murias was brought the Dagda's cauldron. No company ever went away from it unsatisfied.
7. There were four wizards in those four cities. Morfesa was in Falias; Esras was in Gorias; Uiscias was in Findias; and Semias was in Murias. They were the four poets from whom the Tuatha De learned occult

lore and secret knowledge.

8. The Tuatha De then made an alliance with the Fomoire, and Balor the grandson of Net gave his daughter Ethne to Cian the son of Dian Cecht. And she bore the glorious child, Lug.

9. The Tuatha De came with a great fleet to Ireland to take it by force from the Fir Bolg. Upon reaching the territory of Corcu Belgatan (which is Conmaicne Mara today), they at once burned their boats so that they would not think of fleeing to them. The smoke and the mist which came from the ships filled the land and the air which was near them. For that reason it has been thought they arrived in clouds of mist.

To begin our examination of the symbolism contained within these first nine sections I would remind the reader of what I said in the Introduction regarding a change of attitude concerning linear time, and adopting the concept of the three levels.

This opening to the legend is the closest we can get to a Celtic creation myth. All of the world's main religions and mythologies contain some sort of creation myth, the Christian concept of the seven days of creation probably being the most familiar to Western readers, but there is no such clear-cut explanation of creation within the Celtic system. These first nine sections of *The Battle of Moytura* are the closest we shall get to such an idea, as will be explained.

It will be noted that there are three separate races of beings mentioned – the Tuatha De Danann, the Fomoire, and the Fir Bolg. These three races can be equated with the three levels in the following manner:

1. Tuatha De Danann = Spiritual Level
2. Fomoire = Mental Level
3. Fir Bolg = Physical Level

There are also three separate locations mentioned: the northern islands of the world, the four cities, and Ireland. These can also be equated with the three levels, thus:

1. Northern Islands = Spiritual Level
2. Four Cities = Mental Level
3. Ireland = Physical Level

Figure 1:
The Coming of the Tuatha De Danann

It is important to note at this point that these people and places are still all separate and have not yet united into the three-levels-in-one which we have today, and therefore the concepts we are dealing with here exist on a macrocosmic level, and therefore do not immediately apply to our own mundane level. All that has been described so far has occurred on the spiritual level. It is the beginning of creation which, eventually, will become the physical creation in which we exist today.

Section 1

Section 1 introduces us to the race known as the Tuatha De Danann. This title is usually translated as 'The People of the Goddess Danu', and it is the members of this race who are the major characters of the Celtic pantheon. Nearly all of the many hundreds of legends which make up the Irish mythological cycle centre around the Tuatha De Danann and their interaction with our own human race.

Anyone who studies this plethora of myths is immediately struck by the way in which the gods and goddesses are talked about in exactly the same terms as are the more earthly, human characters, and it soon becomes clear that the Celts considered their deities as simply a different form of life, in no way 'higher' or 'better' than themselves or their families and friends.

The terms 'gods' and 'goddesses' are unfortunate in so far as they convey the wrong idea to our modern minds as to exactly how the Celts looked upon these beings. They were not worshipped in the sense in which we use the word today. They were certainly respected and admired, not because they were divine but because they could do things which humans could not do. Similarly a blacksmith would respect a carpenter because he could do things with wood which the smith could not; a warrior would respect a bard who could use words in a way the warrior could not; a builder would respect a leech who cured people of their illness, etc., and so the humans respected the Tuatha De Danann who could perform 'magical' feats which they themselves could not.

It should also be understood that the gods and goddesses, the Tuatha De Danann, were not considered to be immortal, as *The Battle of Moytura* will reveal, but were seen to be subject to the same physical laws, including death, as were the Celts themselves. These subtle but important differences between the Irish Celtic view of deity and that of nearly all of the other religions of the rest of the world, which see deity as superior and immortal, should be kept in mind while studying this magical system.

The translation usually given to Tuatha De Danann, 'The People of the Goddess Danu', is the most commonly accepted one, but it is perhaps wrong in the sense that it does not convey the full meaning behind this race's title. The Irish Celts considered all of their gods and goddesses to be of equal importance and stature, and consequently none were considered to be any better or any superior to any other. Because of this equality there was no concept of 'parent' gods, of *The* God and *The* Goddess, as a lot of other Pagan pantheons believe. In fact the Goddess Danu is a goddess who is not mentioned very often in the Celtic pantheon, and it seems very odd that an entire race has been named after a goddess who seemed to play very little part in their activities, and odd to give her the status of a Mother Goddess when such a concept was unknown and unused by the Irish Celts in the first place.

All of the gods and goddesses had various skills and abilities associated with them; one of the skills associated with Danu was that of craftsmanship. Often within the legends the deity's name is interchangeable with his or her associated skill, and therefore it may well be that a truer meaning of the title Tuatha De Danann would be 'The People of Craftsmanship', or simply, 'The Artistic People'. Judging by the incredibly intricate and beautiful Celtic artefacts which have been discovered throughout the centuries this title would appear to be a very accurate description and a far more fitting one than 'The People of the Goddess Danu', which conveys little and means even less.

It is also worth considering the full meaning of the word 'Tuatha' at this stage. The usual translation is 'People' in the sense of an entire race. This is indeed its meaning, but it should be noted that this term was only ever used to define a rustic or rural people, and used specifically to distinguish the country people from the gentry of the day. The Tuatha De Danann were, in other words, the ordinary folk of the world, like you and me, and this serves to emphasize what was said above, i.e. that the Celts did not consider their deities in any way superior to themselves.

The roots of the word 'Tuatha' also lie in the word for North. In the Irish magical system the North is considered to be the source of all power. It is not surprising then to read that these common people were in the northern islands learning all sorts of magical and powerful arts, for to the Irish listener the word 'Tuatha' would already have informed him or her of this fact.

In the original Irish the Tuatha De Danann are referred to in the plural, 'Tuathai' (a fact which is lost in translation later on), which implies that all of them collectively, the entire race, were in the northern islands of the world. There is no distinction between individuals at this stage, and therefore the information we are being given is to be understood as referring to the race as a whole, on a macrocosmic and spiritual level.

This opening sentence of Section 1, then, tells us that this skilled and artistic rustic race were in the northern islands of the world, the source of all power, learning even more arts and crafts. In addition, these particular arts and crafts were of a magical and occult nature, and were therefore more appropriate to the spiritual and mental levels, as opposed to the skills the Tuatha already possessed, which were appropriate to the physical level.

The text does not make clear whether the Tuatha De Danann had travelled to these northern islands of the world in order to learn the new skills or if these remote islands were in fact their own native homeland. This argument is purely academic and need not concern us, because as I have said, the northern islands of the world are symbolic of the spiritual level, and are not intended to be considered an actual, physical location.

What this first sentence of the legend is saying then is that the ordinary man or woman must look for magical and occult training at a spiritual level and not confine such training to purely physical and/or mental levels. This is emphasized by the fact that the five skills defined in the text are all magical ones, implying that the power of the north, or of the spiritual level, is magic itself, and that this magical power can be attained by ordinary people.

The English translations for these five skills are all very loose, and the words used probably do not convey as much to us today as the Irish words did a thousand years ago. For example, two of the skills mentioned in the Irish are 'Amainsechta' and 'Amaidechta', which have been translated as 'witchcraft' and 'magical skills'. Their true meanings, though, are more subtle, and are closer to concepts such as 'magical frenzy' or 'spiritual trance or ecstasy'. This makes better sense when we consider that the Celts believed they could travel to the spiritual level (the northern islands of the world, as we have it in the text) by means of an Inner Journey in a semi-trance-like state, which could very well be described as a magical frenzy or spiritual ecstasy.

Right from the beginning, with the very first sentence, this legend gives us useful information and instruction – the northern islands of the world/the spiritual level are the source of the magical skills/energy of this world, and the Tuatha De Danann/ordinary man and woman can go there by means of an Inner Journey to receive instruction in these arts.

It must be noted, however, that at this stage all this energy is only potential; it takes a journey to the physical level, represented by Ireland in Section 9, before the potential can be fulfilled and the energy used in a practical way, as in the incident of the burning of the boats. This hints at the fact that the spiritual level and the physical level are in some way interconnected, as is indeed the case. More will be said on this important concept as our examination of the symbolism of this legend continues.

The last part of Section 1 tells us that the Tuatha De Danann surpassed the sages of these magical arts. This tells us that any student of any subject (for remember at this high spiritual level diversification into individual categories has not yet taken place) is capable of becoming better than his or her own teacher. This learning ability must be performed on not only a mental level but a spiritual level as well, for, as we have been shown, it is the spiritual level that is the ultimate source of all knowledge and power. The mental learning capabilities are not enough in themselves but must be tempered with spiritual understanding; a point which perhaps our great teaching institutions would do well to consider today.

As the legend opens here in Section 1 everything is very vague and generalized but at the same time all-encompassing. We are told that all of the Tuatha De Danann are in the northern islands, but we are not given names of any individual people or individual islands. These northern islands are also deliberately called the northern islands 'of the world' as opposed to the northern islands of some specific country or area. We are told that there are sages of the pagan arts there, but we are not told how many, what their names are, or exactly where they are. Everything is in fact in unity, in a great at-oneness, in these deep spiritual realms. There is, however, the potential for differentiation and development, but they can only be achieved by a moving away from the purely spiritual to the more mental and, ultimately, the physical levels. This is what the next part of the narrative goes on to describe. Creation has begun.

Section 2

Section 2 goes on to tell us that 'they' (the original Irish still refers to the Tuatha De Danann in the plural at this stage), studied three magical arts in four specific locations. So from the vague but all encompassing information in Section 1 things are now being narrowed down and made more specific and detailed by the naming of three arts as opposed to the original five mentioned in Section 1, and by giving us the names of the four cities as opposed to the vague location 'the northern islands of the world'. It would seem then that the studying carried out under the sages of the pagan arts is beginning to pay off – the Tuatha De Danann are now becoming more aware of their exact surroundings and are in effect beginning to learn to differentiate and discriminate; probably the two most important abilities of any would-be magician.

Two of the original five skills mentioned in Section 1

have disappeared, which either means the Tuatha De Danann have become so skilled they no longer require any further teaching in them, or that the two skills are not appropriate to this next stage of creation. The two skills which are no longer named are in fact the two I spoke of above, the 'divine trance' ones, and it can therefore be argued that these particular skills are only appropriate to the highest of spiritual levels.

To get to such high spiritual levels, however, the magician in the physical world must undergo exactly such a divine trance while still in physical incarnation which, paradoxically, we have just seen is a state appropriate only to the higher realms. Here we are being given another little hint that the spiritual world and the physical world are very strongly connected.

Do not try to understand this apparent contradiction just yet. The only way you can do so is by applying your logical mind to it, and consequently, you will not understand it. Why should this be? It is the normal Western approach to consider any problem with the logical abilities alone, but to do so is in effect to use only one level of your complete potential. The other two, the physical and the spiritual, are not being brought into the examination of the subject at hand, and therefore you are denying two thirds of your total potential. Clearly no understandable answer will be obtainable under such poor conditions.

Section 2 can be interpreted in a couple of ways, as the text is rather ambiguous. We are told that the Tuatha De Danann, as a whole, studied in all of the four cities, but does this mean that they travelled in a group from city to city, or that all of them were in all of the cities at one and the same time, a seemingly impossible situation?

The answer is that neither of these interpretations is correct. Physical space, the separation between things, people and places, has not yet come into being. The Tuatha De Danann and the four cities are still in the spiritual realms, and therefore, the apparent anomaly does not exist.

What this does serve to show is that the *potential* for separation, physical space, exists at this level, and that we must not fall into the trap of trying to apply our understanding of the physical world to levels which are not of this world. This really is re-emphasizing what was said above about the error of applying logic alone to problems. Clearly we have a lot to learn and to change about ourselves if any of this is going to make sense and become a usable and workable magical system. But take heart, it is early days yet!

Section 2 of the legend is really the transition from the purely spiritual realms of the northern islands to the mental level of the four cities, and is in itself a bit of both. It also prepares us for the importance of triplicities in the Irish Celtic system, in that only three magical arts are described as being studied here.

The following sections, which can be seen as being on the mental level, continue this emphasis on triplicities and also display yet more potential for physical-level existence. Each of the following sections names three specific things – a city, a treasure and a member of the Tuatha De Danann. With this constant emphasis on threes we seem to have hit another problem – why are there four cities and four teachers mentioned? The answer lies yet again in a potential state of being, which is yet to come, but which is being conceived of as a possibility at this higher, creative level. The potential this time is for physical-level *Polarity*, a state which can only exist in the physical level due to that level's unique characteristics of space and separation between things.

This will become more clear once we arrive with the Tuatha De Danann at that level. For the time being it is worth taking a brief look at how the legend presents this concept of physical-level Polarity.

If we look at the four cities as named in Section 2 we see they are given in the order Falias, Gorias, Murias and Findias. In Sections 3 to 7 the cities are named again and we are given more detail about each one, but the order has been slightly changed, with Findias and Murias switching places. This hints at the fact these two cities are closely linked and perhaps even interchangeable. This will occur again later when we come to examine their respective teachers and find that these too would appear to be the wrong way round.

For now suffice it to say that the four cities can be

equated with the three levels of existence as follows:

1. Falias = Spiritual
2. Gorias = Mental
3. Findias and Murias = Polarity of the Physical

For those already familiar with the Western Magical Tradition's use of the Four Elements: Earth, Fire, Air and Water, it should be noted that these can be equated with each city thus:

1. Falias = Earth
2. Gorias = Fire
3. Findias = Air
4. Murias = Water

⎫
⎬ 4
⎭

This may at first seem anomalous. Why should Falias, the spiritual level, be given the symbol of Earth? Again, this is because in the Irish system the spiritual and physical levels are inseparable, one and the same thing. The attributing of Fire to Gorias, the mental level, is quite appropriate, as what better symbol could there be for the fiery processes of the mind and emotions? Air to Findias and Water to Murias are almost self-explanatory when we remember that these two cities combine to symbolize the physical level, for nothing living on the physical level can survive without either air or water.

These associations will become clearer when we look at each city in detail, and especially when we consider the meanings of the names of each city and their respective teachers.

Section 3

Sections 3 to 7 continue the process of further definition and refinement, and are based solely in the mental level. They are preparing the Tuatha De Danann for their eventual arrival in the physical level and the subsequent combining of all three levels into the unity that exists today. At this point it is worth commenting on the fact that the names of the four cities - Falias, Findias, Murias, Gorias - and those of their respective teachers, have caused considerable problems for translators of the text from Old Irish into English. The reason for this is that the suffix -ias is not Irish, and is found in no other known Old Irish words. It is not known exactly how these particular words came to have non-Irish suffixes when their main meanings are clear and definitely Irish, but, in a nutshell, it does not matter, because that is just the way it is!

Some commentators have put forward the hypothesis that the words are actually Latin versions of Old Irish words, the true meanings of which were unknown to the medieval Christian scribes. Others have suggested that the words were never intended to be the names of cities and teachers at all but were in fact adjectives, the meanings of which have long been forgotten. I personally believe that these words are the original Old Irish titles for the cities and teachers, non-Irish spellings notwithstanding. As I said in the Introduction, I believe that the scribes who wrote these old legends down so faithfully took great care to ensure they were accurate and exact reproductions of the spoken version. It is inconceivable that they should have made errors in one of the most important sections of the entire legend. Whatever the truth of the matter the fact is we have inherited the words as given here and we must make do with them.

Section 3 concentrates on the city of Falias. The name Falias means either 'a stone' or 'a hedge', both very earthy objects, which helps to explain why the spiritual level city has the Magical Element of Earth associated with it. We are told it was from Falias that the famous Lia Fail, or Stone of Fal, was brought, and it should be noted that in this and the following three sections the phrase ' . . .was brought . . .' is always used in connection with each city's respective magical treasure. The narrative does not say ' . . .was brought by the Tuatha De Danann . . .', and the implication is that it was not the Tuatha De Danann who brought these treasures through to the physical level but was in fact some other, unnamed agent.

This is highlighted in Section 4 where we are told 'From Gorias was brought the spear which Lug had . . .' yet Lug is not even born until Section 8, and does not make an active appearance in the events of the legend until much later. Some other agent must have been responsible for bringing into physical being the magical treasures which were to play such a crucial part in *The Battle of Moytura* and, indeed, in the magical system of the entire Western Tradition. Nowhere are we told exactly who this agent was. It may have been the four teachers named in Section 7, it may have been the sages of the pagan arts mentioned in Section 1, but whoever it was remains a mystery.

Many pages could be spent speculating over the identity of this mysterious carrier of magical treasures, but, in the end, it does not matter at all who actually carried out the deed. This was a once-and-for-all action, and now it has been done it need never be repeated.

The legend refers to these objects as 'treasures', but they are more commonly referred to as 'weapons' by present-day practitioners of the Western Tradition. Sometimes they are referred to specifically as the Greater Weapons, whose Lesser equivalents are the shield, knife, cup and wand.

They are however a peculiar choice, considering the weapons in use by the Celts at the time this legend was put together. The most commonly used battle weapons were the sling and stone, the axe and the sword. These particular treasures are therefore clearly not intended to be battle weapons, as would have been well known and familiar to the ordinary Irish Celt, but are in fact the tools needed to control and manipulate the powers and energies of the spiritual level from which they emanate. That is, the force of magic.

The stone which was brought from Falias was believed to have been situated in Tara, the spiritual centre of all Ireland and the seat of the High King. This High King was more than just the overlord of all Ireland, as he was held to be the physical-level representative of the spiritual level of all of his people and of the very land itself. It was for this reason that an imperfect king, whether his imperfections was physical, mental or spiritual, had to stand down in favour of a more perfect candidate, as any defect or imperfection in the High King was believed to make itself manifest in all of the people and in the health of the land itself.

This is quite a common belief, and its parallel can be found in the Arthuriad, where the Fisher King is maimed and immediately the land falls waste. This point is demonstrated in *The Battle of Moytura* from Section 11 onwards.

It was therefore vital that the people's choice of High King, which was not a hereditary title as in our present British monarchy, was correct, and that no impostors or unsuitable candidates managed to sneak through. This meant all candidates underwent a lengthy and extensive testing as to their suitability, and the final and most important test of all, was carried out by the Lia Fail itself. All candidates had to stand upon this magical stone. Once the perfect candidate was found the stone would cry out with a scream which could be heard throughout all Ireland. The word Fail may be derived from the two words 'Fo' and 'Ail', which together mean 'under stone' - a very apt description for this magical rock and its function. Students of the Arthuriad will notice the parallel with the parable that only the rightful king will be able to pull the sword from the stone.

When we consider that this physical stone was brought from Falias, the spiritual level, we are again being shown that these two levels are interconnected and, in a sense, are one and the same. This also means that the final test undergone by applicants for the position of High King was a spiritual testing and was clearly the most important both for the applicant and for the people of Ireland as well. Such a test is one which by its very nature cannot be passed by cheats or frauds, nor even by sincere applicants who perhaps do not recognize their own shortcomings. This gives us another piece of practical information - we cannot deceive our own spiritual level, intentionally or otherwise, yet, once it recognizes true spiritual worth, it will make this known on all the other levels.

To use a stone as a symbol for the physical level is clearly appropriate, but it is equally appropriate for the spiritual level. Stone is permanent, durable and unchanging; it is there all the time 'staring us in the face'; and most people look upon it as worthless and simply take it for granted - all apt descriptions for the spiritual level, at least by today's standards!

We can sum up the symbolism contained in Section 3 by saying that it is an examination of the spiritual level and, consequently, of the physical level; the spiritual level is the source of all else, and contains within it the potential for the other levels of being. The information regarding the Lia Fail gives us clues as to how to contact this spiritual level while we are still in our physical incarnation, and highlights the need to strive for perfection on all three levels. We can all take on the status of the High King during our magical workings, but in so doing we must be prepared likewise to accept the responsibilities of the High Kingship – which may include the need to abdicate in favour of a worthier claimant.

Section 4

Section 4 gives us the information we need about Gorias, which, as we now know, is the mental level. The word Gorias means 'fire'. The treasure appointed to this level, the spear, is a very apt symbol for both the mental level and the Element of Fire. Physical fire is best harnessed by means of a long rod or pole, and what is a spear if not such a long rod or pole? The Celts favoured ash as the wood for their spears, and these were hardened in a fire before use. Ash also burns very well, whether old or green. On the mental level we sometimes describe thoughts as being 'far-reaching' or 'straight to the point', both appropriate descriptions of the function of a spear when used correctly.

We are told that this spear was 'the spear which Lug had'. I have already stated that Lug does not yet exist, but in stating that this spear would eventually belong to him we are being given an important piece of information. The spear, which at this stage exists only on the mental level, is destined to be used by a physical-level being who has not yet been born. The fact that this is stated so clearly and definitely means that it is on the mental level that physical-level existence first manifests in a tangible form.

The mental level, as we know, emanates from the spiritual level, so what we are really being told here is that any magical work must first be started on the spiritual level; the magician must then shift his or her consciousness to the mental level, and it is there that he

or she should then create that which he or she hopes to
make real in the physical level. This is the essence of all
magical work; these same stages must be gone through in
this order no matter how large or small the work in hand.

Lug, who will eventually own the spear of Gorias, is a
very important character for several reasons. He is the first
person to be named in the legend, an important point in
itself; he is the first person to be associated with one of
the treasures of the Tuatha De Danann (the Stone of Fal
was associated with a place, Tara, as opposed to a specific
person); he is half Tuatha De Danann and half Fomoire;
and he is the first person to be born into the physical level.
His symbol is the Sun and the Sun can be regarded as the
spirit itself, the fiery processes of the mental level and also
the life-giving warmth so necessary on the physical level.
He is therefore a coming-together of everything on all
three levels, and is an image of the perfection we should
all be striving for.

His full name is Lug Lamfhota, which means Lug of the
Long Hand (or Reach). This name may refer to his Solar
attributes, but it could equally well be a description of
anyone who holds a spear, which does, literally, give the
holder a long arm or reach. We are told that the nature of
this spear was such that 'No battle was ever sustained
against it, or against the man who held it in his hand.' This
tells us that the mental processes used in conjunction
with the spiritual can defeat all problems, and therefore
that whoever fully understands this principle, and can
apply it to the physical level, will be truly invincible.
Another little bit of practical magical instruction.

Section 5

Section 5 now gives us information about the city of
Findias, and not Murias as we may have expected if the
narrative had kept to the order in which the cities were
listed originally in Section 2. Findias is associated with
the Element of Air; the name Findias means 'white' or
'fair', descriptions which could be applied to the Element
as well.

Findias and Murias really have to be considered

together, because between them they represent the physical level, and more specifically the Polarity of that level. This is highlighted in the respective Elements associated with them, namely Air and Water, as these are the two most important things necessary for sustaining physical-level life. We could say that these two cities are literally the vitality of the physical level and all that that level contains.

The treasure attributed to Findias is the sword. Again, this can be seen as a symbol of Polarity, in that the swords used by the ancient Celts were double-edged and designed for cutting things in two. The sword is also believed to be an evolutionary form of the original weapon, which was a short spear or arrow, both of which were projected through the air - our Magical Element again!

This particular sword belonged, eventually, to Nuadu. One of Nuadu's titles is 'Master of the Elements', a physical-level title if ever there was one. Later in the narrative, in Section 11, we shall read that Nuadu unfortunately loses his hand as the result of being cut by a sword; this indicates that the powers of the physical level must be treated with great caution, for they are strong enough to harm even the Master of the Elements. Nuadu's amputation is carried out by a member of the Fir Bolg race, members of which represent the purely physical level, i.e. beings with no mental or spiritual aspect to their make-up. This, as Nuadu learns to his cost, is an extremely dangerous state to be in.

Another Polar aspect of the sword is that most swords are in two parts - the blade or cutting part and the sheath which contains it. It should be noted that the exact wording of the text is 'No one ever escaped from it once it was drawn from its deadly sheath . . .' - in other words, it is the sheath which is deadly and not the sword itself. The sheath, which is the container of the weapon, symbolizes the knowledge of when to draw the sword and when not to - or, to put it another way, when to invoke the powers of the physical level and when to leave them be. Any fool can draw a sword and swing it around, but how many have the knowledge of when best to draw it and, equally importantly, when to leave it in its sheath?

The sheath is also symbolic of the womb and birth

passage, just as the sword is symbolic of the penis, once more these are very physical level associations. The birth passage is also a death passage in so far as the baby being born into the physical level has just 'died' on the Inner levels. Equally, a person dying on the physical level is being born into the Inner levels. Polarity yet again.

This section finishes with the words, ' . . .and no one could resist it', which means that no one, not even the spiritual Tuatha De Danann, could resist the force of the sword or the pull of the powers of the physical level. All beings must go through the same process of being first purely spiritual, then purely mental, and finally purely physical before all three can join to make perfect balance and harmony. This is in fact the whole meaning behind these opening sections of *The Battle of Moytura*, and hidden within this seemingly fantastic fairy-tale are the instructions and information needed to understand these cosmic principles fully and put them into practice.

Section 6

Section 6 can be considered the complementary half of Section 5. In this section we are given information regarding the fourth and final city, Murias. The name Murias means 'the sea', a very apt symbol for the physical level considering it was in the great primeval seas that all life began. The sea is also a vast area of water and, as we have already noted, water is vital if the physical level is to continue to sustain its life forms. It was also by sea that the Tuatha De Danann arrived in Ireland (the physical level), and made life manifest as we know it today.

From Murias was brought the cauldron which would eventually belong to the Dagda. A cauldron is yet another womb symbol; it is also a water container, and both symbols help to demonstrate the links between Murias and Findias and the way in which they combine to represent the physical level and Polarity within that level. Cauldrons were also communal cooking pots, and this implies the ordering of society and the sharing of the good things of this world.

The Dagda, which means the 'Good God', is a very

'earthy' type of being despite his divinity. Later in the text we shall read of his great sexual capabilities and his enormous capacity for eating and passing bodily waste – all very physical-level functions.

The narrative tells us that 'No company ever went away from it unsatisfied.' This could be interpreted on a purely physical level to mean that every one who ate from the Dagda's cauldron was physically satisfied, or it could be taken to mean that nobody ever leaves this world without having gained at least some experience, or satisfaction, which will help and benefit him or her in the Otherworld.

These first six sections of *The Battle of Moytura* have given us an enormous amount of information about the structure and nature of the three levels and how they interrelate with each other, how progress is made from one level to another, where teaching may be obtained, and the symbols necessary for Otherworld journeying, as well as about the physical level in which we have most of our day-to-day awareness, and lastly, about the nature of magic.

These opening sections have dealt with all of the above topics on a grand, macrocosmic level. The rest of the legend goes on to further expand upon these topics, but on a microcosmic scale, demonstrating clearly how these important cosmic principles can be understood and put into effect in this physical level by those who take the time and effort to learn and understand them.

I would suggest that you re-read these opening sections if there is any doubt in your mind as to their full meaning, before you go on to read and digest the following sections.

Practical Work: Preparation

By way of preparation for the actual Practical Work of this book I would suggest that you spend some time thoroughly familiarizing yourself with the basic concept of the three levels, and also with the important notion of time running in a different fashion from the normally held view of so-called linear time.

To do this, spend the next week or so carefully studying the way the three levels can be seen to manifest all around and within you no matter where you are or what you are doing.

Start by doing this first thing in the morning when you awake, even before you arise. Consciously realize that you have awoken not just mentally but physically and spiritually as well. Be aware (which is using the mental level) of your physical body and how it starts to stretch and stir as you become more and more awake. Be also aware of your personal desires and aspirations, beliefs, loves, hates, all coming to mind as the spiritual level – that part of you that makes you different from everybody else – once again wakes up in the same physical and mental body it always has done throughout this present incarnation.

When you go to work, school or play for the day be aware of how all three levels are constantly shifting and changing emphasis, from the physical, when you are doing physical things, to the mental, when you are engaged in thought or perhaps expressing deep emotions, and finally, be aware of that part of you which has most likely been very much neglected in your life so far, the spiritual aspect. Listen, in the periods of silence or quiet throughout your day, to what it has to say. You may well be surprised just how much you start to hear after a little practice!

Finally, on retiring for the night as you lie and wait for sleep, review the events of the day, whether good, bad or indifferent, and try to decide which level was most dominant at each stage of your day and see if you can determine why. From this, test your conclusions on subsequent days when similar situations arise. By doing this regularly you will start to build up a 'reference library' of your own three levels and how and when they affect each other, and with this knowledge you will be much better prepared for the rest of the Practical Work which this book contains.

Just as important is the ability to extend your view of time and how time runs and behaves. For the moment all you need to do is realize that each event of each day throughout the whole of your life has repercussions not only for you but for every other thing in this world and in the Otherworld. These repercussions will also return to you eventually, although in slightly different form, and this can best be symbolized by seeing the passage of time as a spiral, which eventually comes back to the same place it began, but occupies a different level.

The important thing about these exercises, and the ones which follow in later chapters, is that they should become perfectly natural and easy, as much a part of you as everything else in your life is at the moment. You should never need to strain over them, and they should become such a habit that they will eventually be a permanent part of your physical, mental and spiritual make-up.

Chapter 2
Sections 7 - 9

Section 7

In Section 7 of the legend the narrative offers still greater detail, telling us that the Tuatha De Danann are coming closer and closer to the physical level, and that their perceptions are changing with their change of state. This time the specifics we are given are the names of the four teachers of the Tuatha De Danann and their respective cities. We are also told that at this stage the Tuatha De Danann have reduced the skills they are learning to just two, occult lore and secret knowledge. This continues the progression of their learning, bringing about their increased realization and awareness, and also describes the Tuatha De Danann as moving from the purely spiritual level, where five skills were studied, down through the mental level, where three skills were studied and three triplicities were defined, and so to this level, which is the closest yet to the physical level, with its emphasis on Polarity as can be seen in both the form of the teacher/city duality and the fact that only two arts are to be learned.

It is important to stress at this point that these four cities should not be confused with physical locations, nor thought of as being four individual cities situated apart from each other. As I have already said, the separation between places and people has not yet come into being; it is necessary for our purposes, however, to describe these cosmic events in very limited terms, in order for our unprepared consciousness to understand them in even a rudimentary way.

The word 'city' is also a bit misleading, and it may be better to substitute this word with 'place of learning', however one wishes to view such a place. The four cities are in fact four aspects of one cosmic concept, that is, the overall concept of Learning. The Irish system regards everything as being in total unity. Each apparently separate and individual person, place and object is recognized as being no more nor less than one little part, or aspect, of the great cosmic whole. To regard these cities as four separate and distinct locations is incorrect, and we must try temporarily to accept the ancient Irish Celtic way of seeing everything as being in unity and harmony.

It is also from this basic concept of total unity that the concept of the equality of men, women, gods and goddesses originally stemmed, for in any true unity no one part can be considered as any more important than any other. Each is as necessary as the other to maintain the health and stability of the unit.

Just as the meanings of the names of the cities were found to be revealing, so too are the names of the four teachers. In the following analysis of these four great instructors the masculine pronoun will be used, but it must be clearly understood that this is simply for ease of reference, and definitely does *not* mean that these four beings should be considered male. The point is that at this level they have not yet reached physical incarnation, and therefore the splitting into sexes has not yet occurred.

The name of the first teacher mentioned, Morfesa – who was in Falias, the spiritual level – means 'great wisdom', a very appropriate title for one who dwells at the source of all knowledge and wisdom. The word 'great' should be seen in the sense of vast or all-encompassing rather than as descriptive of a degree of quality.

Just as each city should be regarded as a part of the whole concept of 'a Place of Learning', so too should each teacher be regarded as one part of the larger construct of Teaching or the passing-on of knowledge and wisdom, in general. Morfesa, then, is that part of the cosmic teacher that contains all the other parts, just as his city, Falias, the spiritual level, is the city or level that contains all the others. The symbol of Falias - the Stone of Fal - lay at Tara, and Tara was the meeting point of the five divisions of Ireland, and was therefore the heart of Ireland, or that part which contained all the others.

Morfesa can be seen to represent this same unity and at-oneness that we have already encountered symbolically in our look at the other symbols of the spiritual level, that is, the city of Falias and its treasure the Stone of Fal.

The next teacher mentioned is Esras, who was in Gorias. His name can be translated as 'outlet, passage, means, way or opportunity'. He can therefore be regarded as a transition, a way from one thing to another, and not necessarily a final stage in itself. This ties in well with his city of Gorias, which is the mental level, for the mental level can be seen as the way from the spiritual to the physical and back again. The instructions he gives are therefore on a mental, logical and emotional level.

He helps to formulate ideas into abstract forms from their diffused origin on the spiritual level, where they were created by Morfesa, and he passes them on to Semias and Uiscias, who further define them into workable theories and ideas which conform to physical-level laws and principles. Esras is therefore also the teacher to go to when one needs help with reversing this process - the understanding of symbols which are used on the physical level in order to commune with the spiritual level. This is one of the basic techniques of magic, often referred to nowadays as *Pathworking*, and therefore Esras is the teacher to turn to when we seek instruction in the rudiments of magic.

The last two teachers we come to are Uiscias and Semias, who were in Findias and Murias respectively. Just as these two cities of the physical level have to be taken together, so too do the two teachers at this level of existence.

Again, a look at the meanings of their names is very revealing, and highlights the interchangeable nature of these cities and teachers, also re-emphasizing the existence of physical-level Polarity. Uiscias means 'water', and he would therefore appear at first to be more closely associated with Murias (the sea/Water) than with Findias. Likewise the name of his counterpart, Semias, which means 'slender, thin, rarified like air' would appear to be better placed with Findias (white, fine/Air) than with Murias.

The point behind all this switching around is to demonstrate a very important and often neglected principle; one which must be clearly understood by practitioners of any magical system if they are to make the most of their own magical potential.

As we have shown, everything starts its existence in the spiritual realms where, to put it simply, Morfesa conceives an idea for some sort of physical existence, or perhaps maybe change, on the physical level. He passes this idea on to Esras, who refines it and gives it the necessary mental aspect before passing it on to Uiscias and Semias. It is their job to take the now modified idea and give it physical-level existence. Unfortunately the great idea of the spiritual level may not be practical, or indeed possible, on the physical level, and occasionally considerable modifications are needed to the original idea before it can work on this level.

This process can be seen at work in the simplest and most mundane decisions or ideas we have, as we often discover that the original idea we had for a new way of life, a new type of engine, a routine for the day's work, etc., has not worked out in reality exactly as we had planned but has, none the less, been made manifest in this day-to-day world of ours in the only way that the original idea could work due to the limitations of our physical world. This process of shifting and changing to suit the confines and restrictions of each successive level is one which should be familiar to any student of the system known as the Qabalah; it is also the central process of all creation.

Therefore the text is here displaying this cosmic principle by the fact the teachers appear to have deviated from the divine plan and to have been accidentally allocated the wrong cities. It is no accident as we have seen, and as well as exemplifying the principle outlined above it also helps to remind us of the other principle or Law of this level, the principle of Polarity.

The four great teachers of the Tuatha de Danann are also called 'poets' in this section. This is a reiteration of all that has been said above. A poet sets down in words (the *physical* level) ideas and emotions (the *mental* level) which have had their origins in the *spiritual* level. A poet is therefore a worker on all three levels, just as a magician should be, and to use the word 'poets' as the final description of our four teachers is the legend's way of emphasizing this important point before we arrive with the Tuatha De Danann in the physical world itself. As the narrative continues we shall see that both poetry and the power of music were very important indeed to the Irish Celts, and were considered to be quite magical.

It was noted in Chapter 1 that in these opening sections of the legend as set down in the original Irish the Tuatha De Danann are referred to in the plural. From Section 8 onwards, however, the original Irish word used is 'Tuad'; this word is the singular form of the word 'Tuathai', which has been used up until now. Unfortunately the English translation loses this subtle point, and continues to use the phrase 'Tuatha De Danann', or *People* of the Goddess Danu. The importance of this change in the original is that it tells us that the teachings and information given in the legend from Section 8 onwards no longer apply on just an overall, general level, but now refer to the individual reader - you, in other words. The text from now on can be considered a personal teaching manual.

The other important point about this change of reference is that it reveals another cosmic principle: it is only as we get closer to the physical level that the concept of the individual can come into being. Up until this stage everything has been experienced collectively by the People of the Goddess Danu; from now on each experience is individual and personal, and relates to the Person of the Goddess Danu, the reader. For ease of reference I shall continue to use the expression Tuatha De Danann where it occurs as such in the Irish Texts Society's translation I am using, but I will ask the reader to keep in mind that the narrative is really speaking directly to him or her alone from now on.

Section 8

Section 8 is the cross-over point between the purely mental and the purely physical levels, just as Section 2 was the cross-over point between the purely spiritual and the purely mental levels. It gives us yet more detailed information, and even introduces a new race of beings – the Fomoire. No further references are made to the various arts being learned, the cities or the teachers, and we can therefore conclude that the Tuatha De Danann have now completed their theoretical training and are ready to put all this theory and potential energy into practice on the physical level.

The meaning of the word 'Fomoire' is usually given as 'under the sea'. Some scholars have therefore put forward the proposition that the Fomoire were in fact the invading Vikings. We are not concerned here with whether the Fomoire were the Vikings or not, or even if such a race ever existed, for such hypotheses miss the point. For our purposes the Fomoire should be regarded as the race who inhabited the mental level. Up until this point they have existed solely on the mental level, and consequently have had neither a spiritual nor physical aspect to their being. Likewise the Tuatha De Danann up until now have only ever had a spiritual existence, without the other two levels.

Now these two incomplete races have met and have agreed to form an alliance. This voluntary agreement to get together is significant, for it tells us that there was no dispute or undue persuasion on either side, unlike in Section 9, where the Fir Bolg have to be subdued by force. By so allying what has happened is that the Tuatha De Danann have now met, acknowledged and accepted their mental aspect, and likewise the Fomoire have met, recognized and acknowledged their spiritual aspect. We now have a race of beings who are two-thirds complete, needing only physical forms to complete creation.

Several names are given here, both of the Fomoire and the Tuatha De Danann, and all of the characters named play crucial roles in the events described later in the legend.

Balor, king of the Fomoire, son of Dot, son of Net, gives his daughter Ethne to Cian the son of Dian Cecht. This union can be seen as the completion of the joining of the two levels, and it results in the birth of Lug ' . . the glorious child'. This title could refer to his Solar attributes, but equally it may refer to the fact that Lug is the first being to be perfectly balanced on both the spiritual and mental levels and also the first being to be given a physical incarnation. It is important to note that Lug is half-Fomoire, his mother being Ethne, and half-Tuatha De Danann, his father being Cian – the significance of this will become clearer later in the legend. A full examination of the meanings of the various personal names will be given as and when they appear in the text, and any important and relative genealogies will also be examined in full, as it is from studying these aspects of the legend that many otherwise obscure or hidden meanings can be revealed and found to make sense.

Section 9

Section 9 is the most important section of the legend so far, as it is the culmination of all that has happened in the preceding sections and is, in effect, the completion of the creative journey of the Tuatha De Danann from the remote, abstract realms of the spiritual level, down through the more definite and understandable mental level, and into this, the physical level. The importance of this section is also indicated by the way in which specific locations are named, the concept of time is introduced, as well as a third race of beings, and, most importantly, the Tuatha De Danann finally use in a practical way their powers, which so far have only been theoretical. It should be realized, however, that as for any new arrival in this world it will take them some time to master and utilize competently their powers and skills.

It is feasible that Sections 1 to 9 could be examined on their own, and after being studied and meditated on sufficiently could be shown to contain within them the entire Irish Celtic magical system. Fortunately the vast amount of time and effort this would entail in practice is not necessary, as the sections of the legend that follow these first nine go on to explain and demonstrate the main principles of this system in detail, and give as much information as is needed to understand the system's intricacy and how to put the system into effect in one's daily life.

The first sentence of Section 9 is very important, and gives us quite a bit of useful information – 'The Tuatha De came with a great fleet to Ireland to take it by force from the Fir Bolg.' This seems straightforward enough, but if we remember that in the original Irish the Tuatha De Danann are now being referred to in the singular, this opening sentence does not make sense – how can one individual be described as travelling in 'a great fleet'? Surely a single boat would suffice. The answer, yet again, is that there is no contradiction here, so long as we read the text with our minds set on its inner level, and lay aside the apparently confusing outer, or obvious, meaning.

The meaning of Section 9, the information it contains, is aimed at the individual reader, who, as was explained earlier, is now referred to in the text by the use of the singular noun. The subject of this section, however, is still the collective Tuatha De Danann, because they have not yet individually achieved physical incarnation. To put it another way, we can consider the Tuatha De Danann, plural, as being what Jung called the collective unconscious, that great non-physical mass to which we all belong and have access, without losing or destroying our own individuality.

It is important to remember when trying to grasp these abstract concepts that what is being revealed here are 'once-and-for-all' events which occurred on a cosmic level and will never need to be repeated. It is necessary for the reader to be made aware of them, however, and to understand them so that he or she may later comprehend fully the laws and principles of creation, which affect each individual today and which need to be mastered before any magical progress can be achieved.

The second part of the first sentence of Section 9, '. . . to take it by force from the Fir Bolg', tells us that the Tuatha De Danann knew before they arrived in Ireland (the physical level) that its inhabitants would resist their coming. This shows that the arts and skills learned by the Tuatha De Danann in the 'higher' levels have given them the ability to predict the future in a way similar to the phenomenon most people today would describe as clairvoyance but which in reality is far more than that. This also means that for the individual to achieve such abilities he or she must also look to these other realms for instruction and guidance and, if successful, thereby obtain this ability of foreknowledge.

The meaning of the name Fir Bolg is yet another area of constant debate among academics. For our purposes we should simply consider them to be that race of beings who, so far, have existed only on the physical level. We have seen that the Tuatha De Danann started out with only the spiritual aspect to their being, and the Fomoire with only the mental aspect. These two united in Section 8 to produce a race who, at this point in the legend, are in a sense two-thirds complete. The missing third part, the physical aspect, is about to be obtained by the Tuatha De Danann's invasion of Ireland.

The fact that the Tuatha De Danann are expecting resistance from this purely physical level is instructive, demonstrating a principle that affects all of us at some time in our lives - the principle that the physical does not always readily conform to the will of the mental or spiritual levels. This can be seen very clearly in the case of a person who has a strong desire to stop smoking - in other words a mental level action which attempts to affect a physical-level action. The mind is clear and quite set on its objective, but the body puts up a very strong fight indeed.

We must therefore understand that it is by no means a *fait accompli* for the magician simply to carry out the correct workings on the spiritual and mental levels in order to bring about physical-level change. That level may very well put up an independent protest to the powers of the magician; the magician must be prepared for this.

The rest of Section 9 does however go on to demonstrate that it is still possible for the magician to defeat any physical-level resistance. In order to do so, however, he or she must use the self-same powers of that level. The Tuatha De Danann therefore had to incarnate physically in order to dominate the physical level and thereby make themselves complete on all three levels. This is also why it was stressed in the notes to the Practical Work in the Introduction that it is important for the reader to become as familiar as possible with the workings of the Green World around him or her. It is knowing the powers, energies, stresses and strains of the Green World which will help the most in later practical work.

The second sentence of this section introduces a new concept – the concept of time. This sentence starts with the words, 'Upon reaching . . .', a phrase that refers to the completion of a journey, and a journey is no more than a combination of both time and space. Nowhere prior to this section have these concepts been so clearly mentioned; this is because it is only in the physical level that the restrictions of time and space can exist. This is emphasized in this same sentence by the phrase '. . . Corcu Belgatan (which is Conmaicne Mara today) . . .', which has been inserted in the text for no other reason than to highlight this principle of physical-level time and space.

If we consider this point more closely we shall see that it demonstrates another important element for the would-be magician to consider – if the restrictions of time and space apply only to the physical level, then consequently we must be free of them when working in the mental or spiritual levels. This also means that when we are in the mental or spiritual levels we must lay aside our normal conceptions of time and space and accept that they simply do not apply. This has already been demonstrated in Sections 4 and 8 when we read about Lug, who has not yet come into physical existence, and this also explains why I said in the Introduction that it is necessary to lay aside one's normal concept of linear time.

The last part of this second sentence, '. . . they at once burned their boats so that they would not think of fleeing to them', is the first instance of the Tuatha De Danann using their hard-earned arts and skills in a very definite and practical manner. This action has taken place on the purely physical level, and in it we can see the Four Elements being combined to produce physical change:

1. The Tuatha De Danann arrived by sea = Water
2. They landed in Ireland = Earth
3. They burned their boats = Fire
4. This caused smoke and mist = Air

The magical and instructive content of this part of the narrative should be fairly obvious to any person currently versed in the Western Mystery Tradition, especially with its heavy emphasis on the Four Elements of that tradition. There is however another, and extremely important magical principle being demonstrated in this self-same section, one which may not be so obvious to those unfamiliar with the Irish system. This is the principle of being 'in-between', of being neither completely one thing nor completely another.

If we read Section 9 again we should note that the incident of the burning of the boats took place on a beach. What is a beach? It is that area in-between sea and land, being neither completely Earth nor completely Water but a combination of both. The burning of the boats, we are told, produced smoke and mist. What are smoke and mist if not in-between states – smoke is in that unique state of being neither completely Earth nor completely Fire but a part of both; mist is neither completely Water nor completely Air but partakes of both these separate Elements.

Furthermore, other accounts of the arrival of the Tuatha De Danann in Ireland say they arrived during the Festival of Beltaine. Beltaine is regarded as being in-between Winter and Summer, a part of each yet something which exists in its own right at the same time.

This important recognition of the definite state of being in-between is crucial to a full understanding of the Irish system, and as this and all the other important Irish legends unfold it will be noted that many major events are described as taking place on beaches or at fords, that is, places in-between rivers and dry land, and as happening at either dawn or dusk, the two times of the day when the world is in-between day and night, light and dark.

This concept of being in-between may also help to clarify in the reader's mind the difficult concept mentioned earlier, that Polarity actually contains a Triplicity. In this physical level nothing is completely Masculine nor completely Feminine, completely Positive nor completely Negative, each carries a bit of its opposite within it, and this bit forms an independent part, the in-between part. This can be clearly demonstrated by examining a simple wooden stick. It is a complete thing in itself yet it can be given Polarity by stating the obvious fact that it has two ends, a left end and a right end (or top end and bottom end, depending on how it is held!) – but where does one end stop and the other end start? It is impossible to say. It *is* possible to say, however, that it has two ends and a part which is in-between these two ends. Unity can therefore be seen to be composed of Polarity, and Polarity is composed of a Triplicity.

Those of you who can grasp this awkward concept are already well on the way to coming to terms with the Irish magical system. The rest of you, who may still be finding it hard to throw away the incorrect teachings and conditionings of a lifetime, may need to work a little harder in order fully to understand and employ this unique system of magic, but do not despair – there are many, many more examples and instructions contained within *Cath Maige Tuired* that will help you get the most from this very workable system, as the rest of this book will show.

To return to our examination of the legend, we are told in the last part of the second sentence of Section 9 that the Tuatha De Danann burned their boats 'so that they would not think of fleeing to them'. This seems a very strange reason for such a final and irrevocable action, and indeed it can be interpreted in two quite different ways.

Who are the 'they' who might think of fleeing to the boats? Is it the Tuatha De Danann themselves that are referred to here? If so, this would imply that despite their extensive and thus far successful training they are not too confident about the possible outcome of their battle with the Fir Bolg, and have deemed it necessary to cut off their only means of retreat presumably in order to force them to fight all the more valiantly and win the day. Does this mean that at the last moment, when they have finally arrived at the time and place all their work and study has been aiming towards, they lose their conviction and feel they have to force themselves into a situation where they have no option but to carry on?

This may well be what the legend is telling us, for is this not a situation we have all experienced at one time or another? How many of us have read all the books and manuals about driving, have listened to the advice and encouragement of valued friends, have paid close attention to the words of our first official driving instructor, only to find that when we first take charge of a moving vehicle facing on-coming traffic everything we've learned suddenly seems shallow and useless? How many women have carried a baby for nine months and calmly and carefully taken in all that everyone has told them about the proper procedure for an easy birth, only to find that once it actually starts, once the process has become real for the woman herself, all her confidence and preparedness disappears?

Perhaps this is what the Tuatha De Danann discovered, and perhaps unwittingly have left these 'last-minute nerves' for the rest of humankind to experience, too. On the other hand, the little pronoun 'they' may actually refer to the Fir Bolg. Perhaps the Tuatha De Danann burned their boats to stop their adversaries from fleeing the battlefield. If this was so it means the Tuatha De Danann had decided beforehand that this battle would result in the all-out destruction of one side or the other. It was a 'take-no-prisoners' confrontation, and this, as any warrior knows, is an extremely serious decision to take indeed. It implies that prior to their arrival in the physical world the Tuatha De Danann had already decided that all the purely physical-level beings of this world, that is, the Fir Bolg, must be taken in battle. This taking in battle would have the effect of giving the Fir Bolg mental and spiritual aspects to their being, as well as giving the Tuatha De Danann their physical part, and this is in fact what the whole battle is really all about.

This clearly means that the intention of the battle was to affect everyone, both at that time and in all times yet to come, and to have all three levels integrated completely within every living being of this world from that time on. It should be noted here that some of the Fir Bolg did escape the battle. We are not told exactly how they managed this, but they fled to their allies the Fomoire, some of whom inhabited other islands around Ireland, and things therefore did not go according to the Tuatha De Danann's plan. This information is given here to explain why 'incomplete' beings can still be identified today, those people who are so callous and cruel as to obviously have no spiritual aspect to their make-up, for example, despite the fact that we should all be complete three-level beings thanks to the actions of the Tuatha De Danann.

This demonstrates a hard fact which most religions and magical systems do not like to face up to – some people are inherently evil, and will never be anything else no matter how much love, care and understanding is shown to them. Such people are beyond help and should be shunned and avoided. This may sound cruel and in a way selfish, but it is one of the facts of life as described in the Irish Celtic magical system, and is ignored at the magician's peril. This of course does not mean that all apparently cruel or evil people are necessarily incomplete beings, lacking a mental and spiritual aspect, but it does mean that should such a person be encountered in one's daily life the first thing to be considered is what makes this person the way he or she is. If the conclusion is drawn that it is because he or she lacks a spiritual aspect then nothing can be done to help and the magician should not waste time trying to be 'understanding', but should simply accept it as a fact of life that he or she is past hope, and any further contact should be avoided.

This, by extension, also implies that there is a 'flaw' in the make-up of the world as we know it – something went wrong during the execution of the 'Divine Plan' of creation. This idea, likewise, goes against the grain of truth, at least as far as most world religions are concerned, which try to tell us that it was humanity, and not god, under whatever name he is given, that ruined creation. It is, however, a tenet of the Irish system that this world is not perfect; accepting this outlook helps us to make sense of the world as we know it today.

So, to return to the text, whether the phrase '. . . so that they would not think of fleeing . . .' is meant to refer to the Tuatha De Danann or to the Fir Bolg does not really matter, as both answers are plausible. The important point being made in this section is that the three levels were once and for all combined into one composite unity, and have remained so to this day. The implications of this belief are enormous.

What this belief carries with it is the idea that existence as we know it is composed of three aspects, and that these three aspects are inseparable. This would mean that destruction of one level could only ever be successful if the other two were destroyed as well and, therefore, the physical level cannot be destroyed unless the mental and spiritual are destroyed, too. So much for the 'end of the world is nigh' scare-mongering put forth by some people today. It must be remembered, however, that although the world cannot be destroyed it can be changed, and changed perhaps into an environment that is hostile to our form of physical life. In an odd sort of way modern science has put forward this same idea, in terms of matter and energy not being capable of being destroyed but only changed from one form to another. The Celts have been saying this for thousands of years!

Sections 1 to 9 of the *The Battle of Moytura* spell out the basics of the Irish system, and offer enough information to enable the reader to start to put this system into practice in his or her own life and philosophy. It also lets us know that these great events have happened and need never occur again on a cosmic scale – and therefore, all further instruction and guidance given in the legend is of a personal nature and applies to the situations the reader finds him- or herself in within this world.

Practical Work: Exercise 1

The first practical exercise to be tackled is an Inner Journey to the city of Falias. As with all the exercises described in this book, there is no need to force this exercise or to strain yourself unnecessarily either physically, mentally or spiritually while you are performing it. Each Inner Journey is really a connected series of images and symbols which 'speak' to parts of the brain not normally invoked by the routine of day-to-day life. Each of these images and symbols can be considered to be like a little light switch – once it has been 'turned on' in your mind, it will stay there and set off various reactions and combinations which you might otherwise never have experienced in your routine existence.

Like light switches, these images only need to be switched on once. You do not need to keep your finger on the light switch for the light to continue shining and, similarly, you do not need to furrow your brows and strain with concentration over each and every image described in the following text; switch each one on and then pass on to the next one in the order given in the text.

At first there will be many questions and doubts entering your mind: Am I simply day-dreaming, or fantasizing? How do I know this is real and not pure imagination? Is it safe? Am I doing it properly? – all these and other questions besides will occur to you.

This is perfectly normal and, indeed, as it should be. You should never enter into anything new without first questioning it. For the time being, however, all I ask is that you set aside any suspicions or doubts as to the effectiveness of these exercises, and 'give them a go' exactly as I describe them and with as open a heart and mind as you can muster. After two or three attempts at each one, for you should do them often and not just once each, you will start to realize that they have changed slightly and that they are starting to become more individual and personal, unique to you alone. There is a special knack that you will eventually discover, the crossing of the fine line between following the text just as it is described here and, each time you do the Inner Journey, relaxing your mind enough to go with any slight changes that might spontaneously arise out of the symbolism.

Should this happen do not automatically think you are doing it wrong and consciously force your visual imagination back into the scenes as laid out in this book, rather, follow through the change as you see or feel it, follow it where it leads you. There will be times, of course, where such apparent changes are no more than lapses in your concentration, but as you progress you will be able to determine these from the more important Inner changes that occur; this is the way of true development.

This, again is as it should be, for what would be the use of such exercises as a means of personal development if everybody who tried them found the same results and had exactly the same experiences? The descriptions given in this book are meant merely to get you started. After that, with some help from your 'friends', you will be able to experience them as they are best suited to you. For the moment, however, carry out the visualization which follows just as described and try to accept it, for at least as long as it lasts, as being absolutely real.

A Journey to Falias

Before you begin make sure that for the next half hour or so you will be free from interruptions and distractions, and that you will be able to carry out the following visualization without fear of a phone ringing or a door-bell chiming.

After reading this exercise through you may like to make a tape recording of it to play during your first attempts at visualization. This will prevent your having to stop to read the text, allowing you to close your eyes and partake fully of the exercise. Once you have made a few Journeys using the tape recording and have become familiar with the general layout of the Inner scenes I would suggest that you stop using the recording, thereby giving yourself the freedom to let the Journeys take on a more spontaneous aspect which will in turn allow the Inner contacts you make to shape each Journey in such a way that it is new and different, albeit slightly, from any other one.

Sit upright in a high-backed chair with your eyes closed, feet together and hands clasped lightly on your lap. Spend a few moments breathing slowly and easily. There is no need to adopt any specific breathing techniques such as those practised in some forms of Yoga, the emphasis here is on your total relaxation and comfort.

When you feel relaxed and ready, imagine in your mind's eye that the walls and ceiling of the room around you have slowly dissolved away. Instead of sitting in your room you now find yourself standing in a very lush, green field covered in ankle-deep grass. It is early morning and there is a beautiful feel of freshness and vitality all around you, as on a lovely spring morn.

Beneath your bare feet you can feel the earth and the grass upon which you stand. It feels soft and very pleasant, and you are aware of the physical contact you are making with the very earth itself, a feeling usually lost to us because of our need to wear protection on our feet. As you gaze around at the tranquil scene you become aware of many insects in the air around you, some birds singing their dawn chorus in a little copse of trees off to the right, and to the left you see, in the distance, a herd of cows quietly grazing in a field.

As you take in the tranquility and beauty of this scene you remind yourself that although you still feel solid in your body it is a body which now exists in the Otherworld and is not your dense, cumbersome physical body, which continues to sit quietly in this world.

Once the images around you have become as real as you can make them, start to walk forwards through the grass. Try to feel as much of what is happening around you as you can. Eventually you come to a little stream which flows straight across the route you are taking. It is quite wide but does not look too deep, so you start to wade across to the other side. Feel the cool water flow against your legs and feet. Experience the difference between the dry, solid earth of the field and the wet, slippery bed of the stream. As you pass the mid-point of this stream be aware of your mental state rising, as if going up a degree in thought and concentration.

When you get to the other side of the stream you step out once more onto a grassy field. As you walk on you realize that the grass and the soil beneath your feet feel finer, as if of a better quality or grade. The air, too, feels clearer and more refreshing, and this makes you feel quite exhilarated. As you walk on you start to make out ahead of you the shape of a vast city comprising massive and very solid stone buildings, all of which are surrounded by a great wall which seems to encompass the entire city. There is an air of learning, as that of a great university city, coming from the place as you approach the great, open gates set into the massive stone wall.

As you enter into this walled city of learning you find that the streets are very busy with people of all races, colours and nationalities strolling around deep in conversation with each other in every language you can imagine – and more! – and on every topic of science and learning there is. No one pays any particular attention to you; you can go where you please and explore as many streets and buildings as you fancy. It soon becomes apparent that there is a lot to be learned from this place and that many visits will be necessary in order for you to become familiar with its layout and what it has got to offer.

After a while a stranger comes making his way towards you through the crowd. He comes straight up to you, calling your name, and greets you like an old friend. This stranger will appear differently to everyone who treads this path. It may be a male or female stranger, and it is pointless for me to describe him or her. This is your own personal Otherworld friend and guide, and he or she can be trusted implicitly. Ask him (I shall continue to use the masculine pronoun simply for ease) his name and, again, the name you are given will only be known to you and him, so listen carefully! Get to know this person, you are going to meet with him often.

Your guide takes you right to the centre of the city, to a great solid building with a huge doorway. He motions for you to enter but just inside the entrance is a massive slab of solid stone, completely blocking the entrance. Your guide tells you that you must say honestly to the stone why you have come to this place before it will move and let you in.

Think carefully. What are your motives for coming here? Are they good and just, are they selfish, is it mere curiosity? It is useless to try to lie to the Stone of Fal. You must tell it honestly and fully your motives, or aspirations, for being there. If these are acceptable, the Stone silently slides aside and you can enter freely into the great hall.

The interior of this great hall is a vast library filled not only with books but also with screens illustrating all sorts of scenes from life, both past and future. There are also display cases containing specimens of anything and everything you care to mention whether of this world or of the Otherworld. In the centre of this vast repository of All-Knowledge stands Morfesa, the great teacher of the Tuatha De Danann. See him as you will, for he has no actual form and will appear as seems best for every individual fortunate enough to encounter him. Talk to him, listen to him, for he can answer all questions. But be warned - you may not understand all his answers, and you may not like others!

Once you have satisfied yourself that you have achieved all you set out to achieve on this particular Inner Journey (never stay in the Otherworld longer than you really need to), make your farewells to your guide and to Morfesa, with promises to return, and, gently let the scene fade from your Inner view. The scene before you becomes dimmer and dimmer until there is nothing but darkness. Replace that darkness with the image of the room in which you sit and, slowly and deliberately, bring your full consciousness back to this world. Feel the chair beneath you, open your eyes and see the room around you, and gently stretch your stiff legs and back. Once you are fully back in this world you should note down in a diary kept specifically for this purpose all that you saw and did and any information you were given or, perhaps, realized for yourself. This Magical Diary will become very valuable to you in the years to come, so do look after it and keep it from prying eyes. Once all this has been done it is always a good idea to close down all your psychic centres completely by having a hot drink and a light snack to eat.

In the days that follow the start of this exercise you should make an effort to find your own symbolic Stone of Fal, which you will eventually use in magical ritual. This stone, ideally, should be round, flat, eight or nine inches in diameter, and not so heavy that it becomes a strain to hold for any length of time. If possible it should be taken from a river bed or the seashore (the important 'in-between' places) and collected either at dawn or dusk ('in-between' times) and used for no other purpose than as your own Lia Fail. Once you have found such a stone it can be used to rest your feet upon while you are making your Inner Journeys to Falias.

Chapter 3
Sections 10 - 14

The narrative from Section 10 onwards changes slightly, and we should consider the information contained within the rest of the story as being relevant to the individual reader, and not a description of vast, cosmic principles as was the case with Sections 1 to 9. Sections 1 to 9 could be considered in a sense a history of humanity; and because the events of the past have shaped us into what we are today they are still relevant and need to be told. The rest of the legend will now demonstrate how these vast, cosmic principles can be seen to work on our own mundane level, and how a recognition and understanding of these principles on both a microcosmic and a macrocosmic scale will enable us to live our lives to the fullest and to use and manipulate the powers and energies of all three levels to our best advantage.

10. The battle of Mag Tuired was fought between them and the Fir Bolg. The Fir Bolg were defeated, and 100,000 of them were killed including the king, Eochaid mac Eirc.
11. Nuadu's hand was cut off in that battle - Sreng mac Sengainn struck it from him. So with Credne the brazier helping him, Dian Cecht the physician put on him a silver hand that moved as well as any other hand.
12. Now the Tuatha De Danann lost many men in the battle, including Edleo mac Allai, and Ernmas, and Fiacha, and Tuirill Bicreo.
13. Then those of the Fir Bolg who escaped from the battle

fled to the Fomoire, and they settled in Arran and in Islay and in Man and in Rathlin.

14. There was contention regarding the sovereignty of the men of Ireland between the Tuatha De and their wives, since Nuadu was not eligible for kingship after his hand had been cut off. They said that it would be appropriate for them to give the kingship to Bres the son of Elatha, to their own adopted son, and that giving him the kingship would knit the Fomorians' alliance with them, since his father Elatha mac Delbaith was king of the Fomoire.

Section 10

Section 10 is very odd, in that it sums up the entire first battle of Moytura in two brief sentences. It clearly must have been a very great conflict indeed if 100,000 men are reported as having been killed, yet we are given no details at all of any individual acts of heroism or bravery, no descriptions of the warriors' weapons or clothing, and no gory descriptions of battle 'trophies' as is usually the case in Irish legends. The Irish Celts were after all a tribal, warring nation, and their legends tend to dwell at length on battles and fighting. The second battle of Moytura is described in more detail later in this tale, yet this, the first and in a sense the more important battle, is dismissed in two short sentences.

There is almost an air of inevitability about it - as if the Fir Bolg and the Tuatha De Danann knew the battle had to take place and were merely going through the motions despite the fact that both sides knew before the battle commenced that great numbers were going to be lost. Yet in spite of the brevity and lack of detail of this section it does in fact reveal some important occult points.

If we consider that 100,000 Fir Bolg were killed, plus quite a few of the Tuatha De Danann (as Section 12 indicates), we can see that this great battle between the beings of the spiritual level and those of the physical level resulted in many casualties to both sides, and that therefore, in spite of their apparent perfection on the spiritual level, the Tuatha De Danann still suffered terrible losses at the hands of the imperfect physical-level Fir Bolg. This again demonstrates that the physical level is capable of upsetting the best laid plans of the spiritual level and, in extreme cases, actually causing damage at that level.

This piece of information is inserted here to stop the newcomer to such occult matters from becoming too cocky and self-assured, thereby falling into the common trap of believing one level is superior to the others. It also hints at another fundamental and important tenet of the Irish magical system, one which, as far as I am aware, is unique to this system - the dwellers of the spiritual level are as mortal as are the dwellers of the physical level.

As we study the various Irish legends, and in particular *The Battle of Moytura*, we will see that many of the gods and goddesses are killed, and are therefore considered to be mortal. The implications of this of course are that once physical death has claimed the ordinary people of this world they then progress to the spiritual world - but, once there, they can still die or cease to exist at this level just as easily as they could on the physical level they just left. This also means that the Otherworld is not a place of reward or retribution for actions carried out while in a physical incarnation but is in a sense an extension of the physical world, with many of its same trials, tribulations, joys and pleasures.

The main difference between the spiritual and physical levels is that time runs at a very different rate in the spiritual level, rendering the individual immortal in so far as he or she does not age or grow old as in the physical world but appears to remain in a state of perpetual youth. One of the names given to the Otherworld was in fact 'The Land of Youth', and this change in the rate of the passing of time is related in many Irish tales of people going to the Otherworld for what seems to them but a few days, only to return to this world and discover that hundreds of years have elapsed.

This concept may at first be hard to grasp by newcomers to this tradition, as nearly every other religion and magical system teaches the immortality of the soul, usually linking this with concepts of reward or punishment, such as Karma. These beliefs have become so accepted that they are rarely questioned. Whether you accept this viewpoint or not really does not matter at this stage, because, fortunately, we do not have to consider such weighty topics so early in our learning process. Do keep them in mind, though, and think them over. You may well come to the conclusion, as many others have, that the Irish system's belief about the Otherworld is not really such a strange or absurd one after all, and in some ways makes a lot more sense than the idea of the inevitable immortality of what is after all only one aspect of an entire being, with this aspect spending eternity in total bliss or perpetual suffering simply because of the good or bad actions of one brief incarnation.

The main point of Section 10, that the physical level is capable of overcoming or subduing the spiritual level, can be seen at work every day of our physical lives, such as in the case of people who seem to have lost their spiritual aspect completely, due to physical abuses such as drug addiction and alcoholism or mental abuses such as an uncontrollable lust for sexual pleasures or for total power and control over others. Such people have so subdued their spiritual aspect that to all intents and purposes it no longer exists, and the best they can achieve is perhaps some sort of action on their mental level. Their mental level, however, is usually as badly affected by such incomplete lifestyles as is their physical one, and any treatment such people undergo to deal with their addiction, etc. must include therapy for their spiritual and mental levels as well.

The spiritual level is usually still there at least, and it is this factor that helps some addicts and ego-maniacs overcome their condition and eventually get back to a normal, full way of life. The spiritual level will have been badly damaged or weakened during their period of physical or mental excess, however, and it too will require a lot of healing. The Irish system is perhaps the first truly holistic one, and the first to realize the need to consider everyone and everything on all three levels at the same time. The treatment of one to the exclusion of the other two is at best a waste of time and at worse actually dangerous and harmful.

Section 10 names the Fir Bolg king Eochaid mac Eirc;

and we are told that he fell during battle. To the Irish Celts the king represented all of his people on all three levels, and to say that the king was killed really means that the entire race of Fir Bolg were defeated. This after all was the point of the battle - to once and for all totally fuse all three levels of being into one composite whole made up of a physical body, mental abilities and spiritual aspect. This, then, is why we are the way we are today.

Other legends mention Eochaid mac Eirc; from them we know that he was the first king to sit at Tara, and that he was killed by a spear. Tara was the physical-level place which symbolized the entire spiritual level, this is why it was the home of the High King. It was also the site of the Lia Fail which, as we saw earlier, was brought through to the physical world from the spiritual level. By killing the king of Tara, and therefore all the people of this physical world, the Tuatha De Danann conquered this level once and for all. The fact that they used a spear, which as we know represents the mental level, means that all three levels were brought into play:

1. The Tuatha De Danann = Spiritual
2. They used a spear = Mental
3. With which they killed the King of the Fir Bolg = Physical

This progression and use of the three levels is exactly the same as has already been described in our analysis of Sections 1 to 9, but here represented on a smaller, more individualized scale. This progression and use are also the essence of proper magical working under this system, and these concepts must be firmly grasped by the would-be practitioner if he or she is ever to be as successful as the Tuatha De Danann were. It should also be noted that despite the great cosmic concepts being portrayed, and despite the mighty magical prowess of the Tuatha De Danann, they did not actually resort to magic in order to win this crucial battle, but used instead the ordinary weapons and powers of the physical level. Another important point being imparted here, then, is that if there is a 'normal' (i.e. physical-level) way of accomplishing something, then that is the way that should be used; do not automatically resort to magic. Magic, in a sense, should only ever be considered as a last resort, true magic is the ability to use and control the powers of this level successfully without the need to subdue them by enlisting the aid of the other levels.

It may also be argued that technically speaking until the first battle of Moytura was won the Tuatha De Danann were still only two-thirds complete, not yet having physical-level existence, and therefore any magical skills which they had were only theoretical, as full magic must by its very nature partake of all three levels. The Tuatha De Danann had no option therefore but to use the tools and weapons of this world before they could manifest fully here and make use of their full magical abilities. This point is demonstrated later at the second battle of Moytura, which turns out to be a very magical conflict indeed.

Section 11

Section 11 is another information-packed section, and introduces several more aspects of the Irish magical system. It informs us that, as said above, the Tuatha De Danann are not immortal, also several new names are given, practical skills are introduced, and Nuadu's kingship is described as coming to an end.

We have not been told specifically that Nuadu was king of the Tuatha De Danann, but this is implied later, in Section 14. The loss of his hand by a blow from Sreng mac Sengainn results not only in physical injury but also in his having to relinquish the kingship. This was due to the fact that, as was discussed in Chapter 1, only a being perfect on all three levels could represent his people, any physical blemish or disability automatically excluded the candidate from becoming king. Nuadu was also known as 'King of the Elements', and the fact that a Fir Bolg was able to injure him so severely simply re-emphasizes the point made above about the physical level's ability to harm the spiritual level. It also implies that although the Tuatha De Danann are now in the physical level they still have only a rather tentative control over it.

The fact that their king was injured means that the

entire race of the Tuatha De Danann are now likewise imperfect, at least until a suitable new High King can be found, and this is made evident in the following sections, where we shall see that they do not do at all well in this physical world. Later in the legend Nuadu does regain his hand, and therefore his kingship, and the situation described here in Section 11 can therefore be considered a transitional one, and not a permanent state of disarray.

This experience can be recognized in our own day-to-day lives in a variety of different circumstances. For example, we study and learn the techniques of some new skill or ability on a purely theoretical level, we eventually confidently put all this theory into practice for the first time, only to find out that things are not as easy as it seemed they were going to be. We struggle on anyway, determined to overcome these obstacles, and eventually we become masters of our new skills and regain the confidence we had during the theoretical stage.

This sequence of events applies to every aspect of living in this world, and should be borne in mind each time we feel we are having trouble coping or that we are going through a bad patch. Such periods are always transitional, and we must make the effort to carry on regardless.

We know nothing of Sreng mac Sengainn, the Fir Bolg warrior who carried out the maiming of Nuadu. His name may mean something like 'Strong Son of Strength' but despite the fact that he played such a crucial role in the battle of Moytura he appears only very briefly in some other legends, and even in those we are not given any more details about him. The important point is not so much who carried out this important act but the fact that it took place at all.

The next two members of the Tuatha De Danann to be mentioned are Credne and Dian Cecht, a brazier and a physician respectively. There is an important piece of information being given here regarding the nature of the teaching the Tuatha De Danann had in the northern islands of the world. Up until this point, the implication had been that all of the Tuatha De Danann had studied all of the many arts and skills mentioned earlier, yet here we are being told that each had a specialization, an individual skill or ability. They were clearly not all masters of all of the arts but rather each of them individually became a master at one craft or skill.

The relevance of this will become clear later when we examine the passage dealing with the arrival of Lug at Tara, in the meantime, consider it as being advice to choose one craft and stick with it until you 'surpass the sages', and do not try to become a master of all crafts. There is certainly no harm in desiring to find out more about skills or things with which you are unfamiliar, but once you have found the skill or craft which appeals to you, stick with it until you become a master of it; do not waste time and ability by chopping and changing and trying to do and learn too much or too many things all at once.

The point made above, that the entire race was affected by Nuadu's injury, is highlighted in this section when we are told it took two of them, both Credne and Dian Cecht, to effect repairs on Nuadu's hand, and even that an artificial hand was used instead of a replacement of the original limb. It can also be read as implying that the Tuatha De Danann were still beginning to come to terms with living in the physical world, and that they were finding it harder than had been anticipated.

Nuadu's artificial hand is described as being made of silver, and it should be noted that whenever precious metals are mentioned in the text it is an indication that the object or person in question is not of this world but of the Otherworld. This means that the best the two craftsmen of the Tuatha De Danann could do was give Nuadu a temporary repair which involved the use of their magical skills and employed Otherworld material. They had not yet, in other words, learned to use the natural powers and materials of this world. This emphasizes the point made earlier about using the things of this world whenever possible in preference to jumping immediately to magical means and solutions to difficulties or problems.

The two craftsmen Credne and Dian Cecht are brothers, and it is Dian Cecht's two sons Cian and Miach who later manage to give Nuadu back his own hand and, consequently, restore him to his rightful throne. There are a couple of important principles contained within this information. First, whenever we read of two gods doing such and such a thing, or three goddesses carrying out some task or other, we should not interpret it as meaning several people were involved. Rather we should consider each individual named as being one aspect of the task being performed. Just as we said earlier that the four teachers of the Tuatha De Danann are really four aspects of the composite principle of teaching, so too are Credne and Dian Cecht, in this instance, two aspects of the principle of healing.

Second, it should be noted that Cian and Miach, who later effect proper repairs on the severed hand, are second-generation Tuatha De Danann and have therefore learned not only from their own studying but also from the experiences of their parents. This is an important point and helps put into some sort of perspective the very common 'primitive' belief in the power of ancestors and the desire to venerate them. It is simply a recognition of the fact that those who have gone before and who are older have a lot of experience and therefore a lot to teach us – if only we will listen and pay attention. Nowadays our elders are more often than not looked upon as being a bit of a nuisance at times, and as out of touch with 'modern society'. We would do well to remember they have literally years of experience behind them which we can use, learn from, and later pass on to our own children.

Dian Cecht is linked very closely with Nuadu, not only on a physical level as his first healer but also on a higher level as the bearer of the important kingship. We have been told in Section 8 that Dian Cecht's son Cian lay with Ethne of the Fomoire and thereby fathered the glorious child Lug. Cian also helped to restore Nuadu's hand completely and thus gave him back his kingship, and, later, Cian's own son Lug became High King of Ireland for a period of thirteen days. According to another source it was Lug who found Nuadu's original hand (which had been stolen from the battlefield by a hawk) and gave it to his uncle Miach to make good the proper repair of the damaged limb. Clearly the line of Dian Cecht, Miach, Cian and Lug is linked closely with the maintenance of the kingship and all which that symbolizes.

Section 12

Section 12 is another very short passage which reveals a great deal of information when examined fully. We are told that the Tuatha De Danann lost many men in their battle with the Fir Bolg; the meanings behind this were discussed in our examination of Section 10. What is important about this section is the brief list of names of some of the fallen. The fact that we are told that 'many' of the Tuatha De Danann fell in battle, but that only four are specifically named, indicates how important these four must have been.

We know very little of Fiacha, the third on the list. He is not mentioned again in this legend and does not feature very prominently in other legends, but see the notes which follow on Ernmas for details of his parentage and offspring. The fact that we are told so little about him on a physical level, yet he is obviously important, hints at the fact that his importance is not of this world but of the Otherworld, and that it is to the Otherworld we must travel if we wish to discover his real nature and purpose.

The practical exercises given at the end of each chapter in this book will help the reader to make his or her own Otherworld voyages. What will be found there, or how the reader will be treated by the beings of the Otherworld, is not for me to say but for you to find out. The whole emphasis of the Irish system is that of personal involvement and responsibility. There are no priests or priestesses to channel things for you. You are responsible for your own spiritual development and nobody else can do it for you. Therefore on occasion, such as in the case of Fiacha, I will give you enough information to explain how to meet someone or arrive at a certain place, but thereafter you are on your own. This is not a system for the faint-hearted or the lazy, as will be seen!

The first victim mentioned in the list in Section 12, Edleo mac Allai, is similar in nature to Fiacha, and the comments given above apply equally to him. One other piece of information we have is that, according to other sources, a stone was erected at the spot on the battlefield where he fell. This is helpful as it is literally a marker for Otherworld voyages which should help us to identify

Edleo should we chance upon him in the Otherworld. Bits and pieces of information like this are always helpful, as any references to objects, or sometimes animals, being connected to specific people is an indication of that being's Otherworld symbols by which he is recognized. We have already been given quite a few in Sections 2 to 6.

The other two named victims, Ernmas and Tuirill Bicreo, are similarly obscure characters in their own right, although their offspring play absolutely crucial roles in the rest of this legend. Had they not raised the children they did then the whole course of events would have been considerably altered, and the world as we now know it would be a very different place indeed.

Ernmas, which means 'Iron Death', is the first female of the Tuatha De Danann to be named specifically (Ethne, who was mentioned in Section 8, is of the Fomoire). She is clearly of importance. The fact that she is recorded as having fallen in battle also highlights the well-attested historical statistic that Celtic women fought alongside and just as fiercely as their men. This is significant, as it also lets us know that to be a successful practitioner of this ancient system one must adopt the outlook and philosophy of the ancient Celt – and this includes total and true equality between the sexes. Just as the gods and goddesses were considered to be no better than the folk of this world but were simply seen as being different, so too should we realize that man is not better than woman nor woman better than man, but each is equal to, although different from, the other.

From other sources we know that Ernmas was Nuadu's granddaughter, and is therefore closely linked to the kingship, as are all the other members of the Tuatha De Danann named so far. This aspect of kingship was clearly extremely meaningful to the ancient Celt, and it should still be so to us today when we remember the High King's close link with the land. Nowadays any practitioner of this system can rightly call him- or herself the High King, but it must be understood that this association with kingship brings with it the same burdens and obligations which the original High Kings had, including a willingness to stand down should we find ourselves to be imperfect in some way! This will be expanded upon later in our examination of the text.

Ernmas is also linked with sovereignty and the land by the fact that she had three daughters: Banba, Fotla and Eriu, all of whom later gave their names to Ireland, and who are really three aspects of the principle of sovereignty and connection to the land itself. She had three other daughters: Macha, Badb and Morrigan, as well as a son, Fiacha. Macha, Badb and Morrigan are all goddesses of war, or as we should now realize, three aspects of the single principle of war, and thus are also connected with sovereignty and the land, for all the battles in this legend are fought over possession of Ireland.

Ernmas's only son, Fiacha, is the third victim mentioned in this section. This reinforces his importance, which has already been hinted at above.

The final victim named in Section 12 is one Tuirill Bicreo, and he is linked with all the others in that he was the father of Ernmas's children Fiacha, Macha, Badb and Morrigan. It is fitting, in an ironic sort of way, that the parents of the Goddesses of War should be among the first to fall in what was the first battle for Ireland.

Tuirill Bicreo is also known by his other name of Delbaeth mac Ogma (most of the Irish pantheon are known by several different names). His mother was Etan, daughter of Dian Cecht, and his father was Ogma, whom we shall encounter later. He is therefore also very closely linked with kingship through both his maternal grandfather, Dian Cecht (who, as has already been shown, is closely linked with Nuadu) and his paternal grandfather, Elatha of the Fomoire. This Elatha later becomes father of Bres, and it is Bres who succeeds Nuadu as High King. Bres's mother is none other than Ernmas's daughter Eriu.

This rather complicated state of affairs means that Ernmas is granddaughter of the first king, Nuadu, and grandmother of the second king, Bres. It gets even more complicated, for the father of her daughters Banba, Fotla and Eriu is none other than her own son and their half-brother, Fiacha! This very confusing state of affairs helps to illustrate what was said earlier about the genealogies of the Tuatha De Danann being extremely intricate and tangled. By examining these complex and incestuous relationships we can however obtain a much better and fuller understanding of what each deity represents, and thereby learn to work more closely with each one.

Finally, it is worth mentioning that Tuirill Bicreo is father to the three gods Brian, Iuchar and Iucharba, whose mother is Tuirill's own daughter Morrigan. In a different legend these three gods murder Lug's father Cian in an incident which is clearly associated with both kingship and the link with the land which each of us has.

To sum up this very tight tangle briefly we can say that between them Ernmas and Tuirill Bicreo are either mother and father or grandmother and grandfather respectively to all of the most important members of the Tuatha De Danann, those members who later shape the destiny of their entire people and the events of both this world and the Otherworld.

Section 12, brief as it is, has in fact revealed a huge amount of information and has given us enough food for thought to keep us on Otherworld voyages for a long time to come!

For the meantime, though, I suggest that you do not get too involved in trying to sort out the various relationships, but first of all carry on with the rest of this book, following the practical exercises in order. Then, once you are adept enough at making such Otherworld voyages, spend some time getting to know and understand these many different deities. Don't try too much too soon, though!

Section 13

Section 13 is another of the short but very important sections, and, in a way, sums up on a cosmic level all that has gone before. We are told simply that some of the Fir Bolg escaped the battle and fled to the Fomoire, who lived on four neighbouring islands. The fact that some of the Fir Bolg escaped and managed to flee from Ireland is significant, and answers the question that cropped up in Section 9, at which point it was unclear whether the Tuatha De Danann burned their boats in order to stop themselves fleeing or to prevent the Fir Bolg from escaping the battle. It would appear that the Fir Bolg must have had their own means of escape, as this section shows, and therefore the Tuatha De Danann must have destroyed their own boats in an attempt to force themselves on to victory, knowing that they had no means of retreat.

This confirms the point made earlier, that up until the time when they actually put their newly acquired skills and abilities into practice they were still not confident enough in them to cope with and use them successfully. As is always the case with the symbolism contained within this legend, we can see this principle applied on a personal and individual level. This section also tell us that the Tuatha De Danann were not in fact completely successful in their desire to unite all three levels, because they let some of the Fir Bolg escape. This explains the existence of the type of person who has no spiritual aspect to his or her nature at all. It also shows that the ancient Celts realized that there was a basic flaw in this world – a fact that has only ever been considered heresy by the major religions of the world.

A greater principle is completed in this section, however, and that is the final conjoining of the three levels, symbolized by the interactions between the three races involved. In Section 8 the Tuatha De Danann mated with the Fomoire, in other words, the purely spiritual acquired a mental aspect to its being; in Section 10 the Tuatha De Danann battled with the Fir Bolg and won, that is to say, the two-thirds complete Tuatha De Danann acquired the necessary third part, the physical level, to make them whole. Now the survivors of the battle are fleeing to their Fomorian allies, or to put it another way, the physical aspect is desperately seeking its mental aspect. Later still, the Fomorians make war on the Tuatha De Danann, which is the circle turned 180 degrees.

It has been stressed throughout our examination of this ancient symbolism that the events described so far happened once only and need never happen again. Now that they have happened, creation has occurred and we are all three-level beings and therefore complete. If this is the case, then it is a fair question to ask why is there so much fighting that goes on later in the legend between these three races? The answer to that is obvious if we stop for a moment and consider the world around us. Is it not a constant battlefield? Has there ever been a time in the history of the world when there was not fighting going on in some corner of it? This of course applies equally well on an individual basis, where we find one level is constantly trying to dominate or subjugate the other two. The Irish system recognizes this harsh fact of life, and it is this inescapable principle that is demonstrated here.

Like it or not we live in an imperfect world, and as long as the world is imperfect so too shall we be. It is possible, however, to step outside the effects of this constant planetary and personal fighting. This is symbolized later in the legend when a perfect being arrives on the scene and takes charge of events. On a magical level we could say that what this symbolizes is that every man and woman can rise above such things, but that he or she must do so on a very personal, individual level. We can help each other to a certain extent, as hopefully this book is doing for you right now, but at the end of the day it is only sheer effort on the part of the individual that will eventually win through. Some will win, as did the Tuatha De Danann, some will fail, as did the Fir Bolg who escaped the battle, and some will make some progress but eventually fall away, as did the Fomoire.

This may seem harsh and even contrary to the esoteric teachings that the reader has come across before but, in my view, it is much more realistic and reflects accurately the state of the world we live in today, unlike some of the rather flighty ideas put forward by other systems and traditions. It also places the burden of self-advancement fairly and squarely on the shoulders of the seeker and, if things go wrong, he or she has only him- or herself to blame. It is not an easy option, and there are no scapegoats to blame, but, as has been said, this is a far more realistic approach to life and its problems than the attempt to achieve some high spiritual goal which is simply unobtainable.

The naming of four identifiable islands in this section tells us that events are now quite definitely taking place in this world, and that the whole process of creation and coming into being has clearly been completed. These four islands must have had very special significance for the ancient Celts if they are given such an important place in the telling of this legend, and indeed we know that the first island mentioned, Arran in the Firth of Clyde, was considered to be the physical-level manifestation of the Otherworld, and that according to other legends it was on Arran that Lug was educated until he earned the title of 'Master of all Crafts'. Clearly Arran must have been considered a very important centre of learning as well as being the Otherworld itself. Because the Otherworld had this physical location it would therefore be possible to visit it before death; the purpose of such a visit would be to learn. Time passed at a very different rate in this Otherworld, and the student could learn a great deal indeed during the passage of only an insignificant amount of this-world time. This again is an important bit of information, as it tells us that instruction and training, on any subject, is best sought in the realms of the Otherworld. More will be said about this later.

Section 14

So far the emphasis in the legend has been on entire races as opposed to individuals, but from Section 14 onwards this changes and we begin to get details of characters whom we can get to know and to whom we can relate. This section is concerned with choosing a new king, as '... Nuadu was not eligible for kingship after his hand had been cut off'. This statement re-emphasizes the point made earlier, that the king of the Tuatha De Danann had to be perfect in order to represent the spiritual aspect of his people and the very land upon which they lived and worked.

The statement is slightly ambiguous, as it could mean either that Nuadu had already been king but now had to stand down in favour of another or that he had only been merely a contender, presumably along with others, for that title. Either way, the Tuatha De Danann now find themselves in the position where they must choose a king, with all that that implies. This clearly indicates that they are now firmly rooted in this world, realize the need for a king, and, on a more basic level, are now having to make decisions for themselves.

This emphasis is shown in two ways: 1) the text now refers to them as 'the men of Ireland' (i.e. the physical level) and not as the 'Tuatha De Danann' as has been the case up until now, and 2) the indication of Polarity, a physical-level phenomenon, by the use of the phrase 'their wives'. The use of the word 'wives', as opposed to, say, 'women', makes it a much more personal issue, as a wife can be considered the feminine aspect of a man just as a husband is the masculine aspect of a woman. The fact that there was 'contention' between the men and their wives indicates the continual struggle between the opposites of any Polarity on this level.

This contention between man and wife, as the text has it, has far-reaching results; a piece of practical information is being given here as well, on what may be considered nowadays as a very mundane matter – the importance of understanding and recognizing the stresses and strains that occur in any partnership, especially a marriage. The result of any marriage is not just the coming together of a man and woman but also the creation of a third facet, which we know as the give-and-take, pleasure and pain – all the spiritual, emotional and physical things which cannot occur to an individual alone. This is the third aspect of Polarity, as mentioned in Chapter 2, demonstrated in a very concrete way.

Understanding that there is a third, almost independent aspect to a marriage, or indeed to any formal, recognized partnership or friendship, is vital if any success is to be made of it. Too often this important issue is missed or ignored, and a true uniting of the two partners never actually takes place.

Later in the text we shall see what can happen in an unsatisfactory situation such as this, for as a result of the contention between the men of Ireland and their wives a bad decision is reached, which makes for a disastrous start to their new life in Ireland, a life the Tuatha De Danann had been looking forward to for so long.

The fact that the contention concerns the new king is a very delicate situation for the Tuatha De Danann. A wrong decision now would have far-reaching effects, not only for the people themselves but for the very land and, as they are now beginning to realize, correcting such a wrong decision will be very hard due to the limitations and restrictions inherent in the physical world. Eventually it is the wives who make the suggestion which is subsequently adopted, and this indicates the importance of paying attention to the feminine, intuitive side of one's nature, whether you are male or female, and not always leaving the decision-making up to the more masculine, logical aspect of oneself.

A subtle but important point is brought up in the phrase, 'for them to give the kingship to Bres'. It is the people who are the custodians of the kingship, and therefore of the sovereignty, the land and their own spiritual aspects, and it is the ordinary people's right to give, or deny, kingship. The idea of kingship being won by force, or by accident of birth, does not enter into the Irish system, and it was always the people who chose the candidate they felt most suitable. The final test was of course the Lia Fail: if it screamed, then all would be well, if not, then another choice had to be made.

The eventual choice is for Bres, son of Elatha, a member of the Fomoire, and of Eriu, Ernmas's daughter and a member of the Tuatha De Danann. The choice of a half-Fomorian to take the Tuatha De Danann kingship may at first seem a bit odd, but this paradox is explained by the description of him. He is called 'their own adopted son'. Adoption and fosterage were two very important institutions to the Celts, and children paid more respect to and had a closer bond with foster parents than they had with their natural parents. This practice of adoption and fosterage was used very successfully to forge links not only between individual families but also whole tribes and peoples, as this section demonstrates.

The other important point in this section is that if Bres was 'their own adopted son' he must have been among the Tuatha De Danann for some time. We have already noted that he is part Fomorian and, therefore, he must have gone with the Tuatha De Danann when they conjoined with the Fomoire to produce Lug (see Section 8, page 24), as there has been no other contact between these two races since that time. It may well be that some sort of exchange took place at the time when Lug was taken to Arran (the Otherworld) for instruction and Bres was brought over to

Ireland (the physical world) to live with the Tuatha De Danann. Bres and Lug can therefore be considered complementary to one another - Polarity again - and clearly are closely linked in a very strong and magical way. This will become more clear as the story unfolds. Bres can be considered to be Lug in reverse, since it is Lug's father who is of the Tuatha De Danann and his mother who is Fomorian, and this reversal is yet another manifestation of the original reversal discussed in Sections 6 and 7 and concerning the placing of Findias and Murias.

By making Bres king the alliance between the Fomoire and the Tuatha De Danann is made even stronger. His father is Elatha, king of the Fomoire, and his mother is Eriu of the Tuatha De Danann, one of the goddesses of sovereignty. His grandparents are therefore Delbaith (or Tuirill Bicreo) and Ernmas, who, as has been stressed, are inextricably linked with the current and future sovereignty of Ireland and with the fate of the Tuatha De Danann as a whole. He is therefore a most obvious choice and, on the surface, would appear to be potentially a perfect king.

As the text continues, however, we shall see that Bres is far from being a good ruler, and herein lies an important bit of information for the reader. Despite a person's ancestry, ability, training or whatever, at the end of the day that person is still an individual and will act and behave as he or she sees fit and not necessarily as expected or predicted to do. Therefore, never judge a person by his or her pedigree, past actions, abilities or any other 'historical' aspect of character.

Sections 1 to 14 can be regarded as a creation myth in so far as they describe the coming into being of the inhabitants of this world and of the Otherworld, on all three levels, and the setting up of the stresses and energies that give both worlds and all levels their vitality and power. It should be noted that this creation myth is not concerned with how the whole planet came into being, as most of the world's creation myths are, but concentrates solely on people, disregarding the places.

This stems basically from fact that the Celts believed that the world simply had always existed; precisely how it came into being was irrelevant to them, as the only thing that mattered was the here and now. The creation with which this myth is concerned is the creation of the individual and his or her development, and the energies, stresses and strains that exist within and between us all. The principles that the legend describes allegorically in the goings-on of the Tuatha De Danann, the Fomoire and the Fir Bolg are still valid and relevant; they continue to apply as much to the modern reader as they did to the Irish Celt two thousand years ago.

Practical Work: Exercise 2

A Journey to Gorias

Our next exercise takes us on an Inner Journey to the city of Gorias, where we shall make contact with the teacher, Esras.

Start as in the last exercise by eliminating the risk of interruption, sit quietly and breathe regularly for a few moments before allowing the room in which you sit to dissolve away in your visual imagination. The scene which unfolds before you is almost the same as in the last exercise, although this time you notice immediately that the setting is much brighter, as if it is midday in summer, and the earth beneath your feet feels quite warm. The grass in the field is parched, and there is a general feeling of warmth, dryness and high summer.

As before, walk on until you reach the stream that flows through this meadow. This time, however, it has dried up to barely a trickle, and the water is warm about your feet as you step through it to the other side. Be aware of your consciousness rising as you step out onto the parched ground at the far side of the little stream.

As you walk forward the city of Gorias starts to come into view. Unlike Falias with its huge stone buildings and great stone wall, this city looks very Mediterranean, with its small, square, whitewashed houses and the dry, dusty cobbled streets between the haphazard rows of buildings. The streets are busy with many people, who also look Mediterranean. They are going about their business, and here and there you see open cafes where people are talking and arguing constantly, as if in some sort of permanent great debate.

Soon, pushing his (or her) way through the throng, your guide comes toward you, motioning with his hand for you to follow. You make your way through the streets until they converge on a great square in the centre of the city. Standing in this square is a solitary building which looks almost like a Greek temple but is subtly different, and you cannot help but notice that its walls are covered with hundreds of different signs, *sigilla* and symbols.

You climb the few steps towards the entrance, but there barring your way is an enormous figure who seems to radiate light and heat. In his grasp is a huge, fiery spear, which he lowers slowly and points at you, daring you to come any closer. He stares at you silently for a moment, and then in a great voice booms out, almost as if from inside your own head,

'Tell me why you believe I should let you enter my place of learning.'

Think carefully before you answer, for your reply must be an honest one and an acceptable one. You must be fully confident not only in your own abilities for undertaking these Inner Journeys but in your true motives as well. Those who try to make such journeys for the wrong reasons, even though they may be sincere in heart, will spend their time in no more than idle day-dreams. Those of you, however, who are beginning to understand this system, and understand yourself, will start to learn and experience a great deal from them.

On receiving an acceptable reply, Esras steps aside and allows you to enter his place of learning. Inside it is very hot, and the walls, floor and ceiling are covered in many different symbols. Some are mathematical, others are letters which you recognize; some are astrological and others are alchemical but, wherever you look, there are more and more drawings and squiggles. Esras, who seems to have shrunk in stature in order to fit into this room, follows you, and now you can ask him to explain any of the symbols which you see but do not understand, and likewise, you can ask him about any topic relating to magic and Inner Workings about which you seek guidance or clarification. Listen carefully to his replies, but do not expect them always to be in words - he may decide an answer can be better given in the form of a new symbol. Note carefully all he says and shows you and, when this journey has finished, remember to make a note of it in your Magical Diary, even if you do not understand them at present.

Once you have conversed long enough with Esras, close down the session in the way described in Exercise 1, and again have a drink and something to eat after writing up your experiences in your Magical Diary. Remember, you can return to Gorias and Esras whenever you like should you have any further questions or queries. Now that you are learning the techniques for contacting such helpful beings – make use of them!

During the days in which you are doing the above Inner Journey you should also be on the look-out for a suitable wand (the magical equivalent of the Fiery Spear). At this stage a lot of novices are tempted to carve some large, elaborate and long staff for themselves, which no doubt looks very impressive but which in reality is useless. The wand represents the *Will* of the magician, and you should bear this in mind when deciding on exactly what your wand will look like. It will also need to be used during ritual workings and, with this in mind, it is easy to see that a short, easily handled wand is much more practical than a great long pole which is cumbersome and liable to knock both people and objects over as soon as it is lifted from ground level. Certain woods are considered to be better than others for making spears; in the Irish system these are yew, ash and rowan. I would suggest that of these ash is the best, as it is easy to find, tends to grow straight, and is not poisonous!

Chapter 4
Sections 15 - 23

From Section 15 onwards the narrative seems to change in direction and style, and this has lead some of the people who have written about and researched these ancient works to believe that what we have inherited from the past is corrupt, and no more than several unconnected pieces that somewhere along the line have been joined together haphazardly and in a manner that was never intended originally. If we accept this view there is no point delving any deeper than the surface meaning of each individual legend. However, once we adopt a viewpoint that is as close as we can manage to that of the ancient Irish Celt, we can see that these works actually do contain a great deal of practical instruction and information, and we find that the question of whether the text was originally a collection of separate pieces or not is irrelevant - their meaning remains valid.

If the legends are indeed a jumble of originally separate pieces, what guiding hand helped them to be joined together in the way we find them now? Perhaps the gods and goddesses had a major influence in the 'haphazard' placing of the disjointed pieces, for, as we begin to see, the pieces do make sense and are helpful despite their apparently rambling nature.

15. Now the conception of Bres came about in this way.
16. One day one of their women, Eriu the daughter of Delbaeth, was looking at the sea and the land from the house of Maeth Sceni; and she saw the sea as perfectly

calm as if it were a level board. After that, while she was there, she saw something: a vessel of silver appeared to her on the sea. Its size seemed great to her, but its shape did not appear clearly to her; and the current of the sea carried it to land.

Then she saw that it was a man of fairest appearance. He had golden-yellow hair down to his shoulders, and a cloak with bands of thread around it. His shirt had embroidery of gold thread. On his breast was a brooch of gold with the lustre of a precious stone in it. Two shining silver spears and in them two smooth riveted shafts of bronze. Five circlets of gold around his neck. A gold-hilted sword with inlayings of silver and studs of gold.

17. The man said to her, 'Shall I have an hour of lovemaking with you?'

    'I certainly have not made a tryst with you,' she said.

    'Come without the trysting!' said he.

18. Then they stretched themselves out together. The woman wept when the man got up again.

    'Why are you crying?' he asked.

    'I have two things that I should lament,' said the woman, 'separating from you, however we have met. The young men of the Tuatha De Danann have been entreating me in vain - and you possess me as you do.'

19. 'Your anxiety about those two things will be removed,' he said. He drew his gold ring from his middle finger and put it into her hand, and told her that she should not part with it, either by sale or by gift, except to someone whose finger it would fit.

20. 'Another matter troubles me,' said the woman, 'that I do not know who has come to me.'

21. 'You will not remain ignorant of that,' he said, 'Elatha mac Delbaith, king of the Fomoire, has come to you. You will bear a son as a result of our meeting, and let no name be given to him but Eochu Bres (that is, Eochu the Beautiful), because every beautiful thing that is seen in Ireland - both plain and fortress, ale and candle, woman and man and horse - will be judged in relation to that boy, so that people will then say of it, "It is a Bres." '

22. Then the man went back again, and the woman

returned to her home, and the famous conception was given to her.

23. Then she gave birth to the boy, and the name Eochu Bres was given to him as Elatha had said. A week after the woman's lying-in was completed, the boy had two weeks' growth; and he maintained that increase for seven years, until he had reached the growth of fourteen years.

Section 15

The brief and simple statement given in Section 15 is a form of marker, and you may have noted that the main points within Sections 1 to 14 - concerning the creation, learning and coming into being of the Tuatha De Danann - are repeated in these sections on an individual basis as symbolized by Bres. The creation myth of the opening sections was on a grand, macrocosmic scale, which slowly narrowed down to an individual scale as described in Section 14. Now with these sections the whole creation process is being repeated, only this time it is played out on a personal, microcosmic scale. In the latter part of the legend the themes spread outwards and upwards again to encompass the whole of creation on all three levels of being, thereby completing the eternal cycle of birth-life-death and re-birth.

This illustrates that the physical and spiritual levels are interwoven, and that whatever principle can be applied to the individual can likewise be applied to the rest of creation and vice versa. The legend therefore can be split into three (always three!) sections, dealing first with macrocosmic creation, then with microcosmic creation, and then with a return to the theme of macrocosmic creation. Thus is the cycle through the three levels to which everything and everyone is subject completed.

This may at first seem unnecessary repetition, but the reason for my constant emphasis on this one point is to highlight the way everything works and evolves, no matter which level is being scrutinized. It also of course reveals the underlying concept of reincarnation. I said earlier that death occurs not only on the physical level but also on the

Figure 2:
Eriu Sees Elatha

spiritual level, and that a death on one level is simply a birth into another. Physical death results in a spiritual birth, a spiritual death results in a physical birth. An understanding of this principle will help to open up the many meanings contained within this and other Irish legends, and will help to clarify passages which otherwise will be rather confusing.

It should also be remembered that in the Irish system there is no concept of sin or Karma, and reincarnation therefore has nothing whatsoever to do with the Eastern concept of debts or rewards being balanced out in future lives.

Section 16

The importance of the feminine, as discussed in Section 14, is re-emphasized now in Section 16. The main character here is Eriu, daughter of Delbaeth and one of the queens of sovereignty. She is the spiritual aspect of the triple Goddess of Sovereignty, the other two aspects being her sisters Banba and Fotla, and the fact she is described as 'the daughter of Delbaeth' and not '*a* daughter of Delbaeth' emphasizes the fact that the three sisters are as one.

We are told that she was in a house and was looking at the sea and land. Section 22 implies that this house was not her own home; she therefore must have travelled there for some specific reason or purpose. This house is in fact in the Otherworld, as the appearance of her glittering companion later confirms. In modern Western Mystery Tradition terminology we would say she is undertaking a Pathworking, or, more simply, that she has raised her consciousness to the next level of being. The sea and land were already introduced, on a cosmic scale, in Section 9; they are re-introduced here on a more mundane level.

The meaning behind all this can be summed up as:

1. Eriu, Goddess of Sovereignty = the Spiritual Level
2. She is in an Otherworld house = the Mental Level
3. She gazes upon the sea and the land = the Physical Level

All three occur at the one time, and while she is still in physical incarnation - a perfected state indeed. The following sentence starts with a statement indicative of time: 'After that, while she was there', and we can conclude from this that Eriu was in a timeless, meditative state as she gazed upon the calm scene before her.

The harmony which she was experiencing, the feeling of everything being balanced and calm, is interrupted by something coming into view, symbolic of something interrupting her meditations - a common enough experience! This interruption is caused by 'a vessel of silver . . . on the sea'. As said earlier, references to precious metals in these legends indicate the appearance of an Otherworld person or object. The fact that this is a silver boat arriving on the sea can therefore be read as an Otherworld idea manifesting in Eriu's own, mental level.

Of this silver vessel we are told 'Its size seemed great . . . but its shape did not appear clearly . . . and the current of the sea carried it to the land.' This means that during Eriu's meditations a vast new idea or concept came to her, the exact nature of which eluded her at first. This vast idea or concept is symbolized by the silver vessel, and silver itself is reflective, indicating that further reflection and meditation will be necessary in order to understand whatever this Otherworld idea is. The 'current of the sea carried it to land', which means it came through to full consciousness as opposed to remaining unformed in her subconscious.

It is therefore one of those rare ideas or concepts that come to mind during meditation, apparently from nowhere, and later have a profound effect on the life of the thinker. Considering that the one meditating is in this case Eriu, the spiritual aspect of Ireland itself, we can begin to get an indication of the enormity of this new idea or concept; this is further implied in the text by the way in which the vessel is described as 'great'.

The next paragraph of Section 16 is interesting, starting as it does with the sentence, 'Then she saw that it was a man of fairest appearance.' Note that the text does not say she saw that the great vessel contained a man but that the great vessel *was* a man. This shows that further meditation and reflection upon the initially vague idea, symbolized by the great silver vessel, has narrowed it down a bit and made it clearer and more specific. Anyone who is already familiar with the techniques of meditation will realize the truth behind this description - what comes to mind initially during meditation usually turns out to be something quite different by the end of the session.

This man of fairest appearance can be considered symbolic of Eriu recognizing her own Polarity, her own masculine side. The fact that he is described in very flowery, favourable terms is what normally happens in the descriptions in these legends of such important situations. Psychologists today talk of exactly the same thing in terms of the Anima and the Animus. The use of metallic colours to describe him, and the exclusion of any other descriptions of colour, demonstrates Eriu's intuitive recognition of just how important this complementary half of herself is - and, of course, the fact that he has an independent existence of his own in the Otherworld. The fact that he is a warrior, well-equipped with very elaborate and intricately decorated arms, emphasizes his attributes of strength and power.

This warrior can therefore be regarded in two ways - he is the masculine aspect of Eriu (and therefore of Ireland), and he is a dweller in the Otherworld. Despite the fact he is at this stage portrayed symbolically as a part of Eriu, we shall see later in the text that he does have a very real and independent existence in his own right. This introduces a subtle but important piece of practical information - ideas or concepts realized during meditation often later work themselves out and eventually manifest in one way or another in the physical world. This means that the period following such a meditation session is just as important as the meditation itself, and attention should be paid to people and events which may indicate the subsequent physical manifestation of the ideas come upon during the mental part of meditation. This latter stage could, in a sense, be described as the physical part of meditation - a part which is often forgotten or simply not considered.

Section 17

Section 17 displays the principle outlined above in that it describes the final stage of Eriu's meditations and brings into physical being all which has gone before. The warrior's questions indicate his desire to join with Eriu on a physical level – he desires this because he knows he must experience her just as she must experience him in order to achieve the necessary balance between their separate Polarity. The fact that he requests 'an hour of lovemaking' as opposed to, say, a permanent marriage, shows that such a conjoining, no matter how long or how brief, is a once-and-for-all matter, which once completed can never be undone.

This principle is obvious on a purely physical level, but it should be remembered that this once-and-for-all principle applies equally to the other two levels. To recognize one's own opposite half, or Polarity, and to accept and join with it results in a permanent change in the individual, and is an irreversible act.

Eriu's reply to the warrior indicates that she does not yet recognize him; this can be interpreted in two ways. Either she does not know him because she has never before encountered her own masculine half, or she does not know him because he is an independent Otherworld being. His reply to her statement, 'I certainly have not made a tryst with you,' is the simple and obvious one. It does not matter if they know one another or not, the deed must be done and that is all there is to it.

Section 18

From the next section it is clear that Eriu agrees with this point of view and goes ahead with the lovemaking, regardless of any previous proposals, or lack of them, from the men of her own people, the Tuatha De Danann.

Section 18 tells us that once the lovemaking is over Eriu starts to weep, and that the stranger asks why. This weeping could indicate sorrow or regret on Eriu's part, and if so, this is the first time negative emotions have been introduced to the narrative. This is in fact the best place to bring up these negative human emotions, as we are considering intimate events described from a human, emotional point of view, and in a way they are the negative, balancing aspect of the so far very positive emotions that have been described in the text.

The warrior asks her the reason for weeping and she gives two reasons – she is scared she may lose him now the lovemaking is over, and she has given herself to a stranger despite the fact her own people, the Tuatha De Danann, had been entreating her before he came on the scene. It would seem then that one of the results of her joining with her own complementary half is the arousal of her emotional level – a negative emotional level at that. One of these negative emotions is the fear of loss, the fear that this important part of her may be taken away even though she has only just become aware of it. Fortunately the stranger's reply in the following sections assures her that this will not happen and, indeed, it is impossible anyway.

This situation is one which we have all experienced, no matter how briefly, where a realization concerning ourselves has brought with it a moment's panic – perhaps the realization is wrong, perhaps whatever has been revealed will later be taken away. The same principle is manifest and can also be experienced in the very common situation where, immediately after being given a piece of very good news, our first reaction is to say, 'It cannot be true, things like that don't happen to me!'

This section is really putting forward the same principles as described, in a slightly different form, in the Biblical story of Adam and Eve and the events surrounding their expulsion from the Garden of Eden.

It should also be realized that the stranger is likewise learning and gaining knowledge and experience from Eriu, and we should not make the mistake of looking upon such Otherworld characters as being all-knowing, constantly correct indicators of 'the way'. Such beings have to learn and evolve just as Eriu does.

Section 19

Section 19 contains a motif common throughout the Irish legends – the giving of a ring in token of future recognition. The section starts with the stranger assuring Eriu that her anxiety about his going away, and her rejection of her own people, will be removed, yet paradoxically he does go away and she does reject her own people. What has happened, in other words, is that the stranger does as he promises he will – he removes her anxiety about these events. He does not, however, prevent the events themselves taking place. This is a very subtle but important point. In day-to-day terms what this means is that unpleasant and unwanted things are going to happen to us throughout our lives, and nothing we can do will prevent them. What we can do is change our reactions to such unwelcome occurrences, and this, if done properly, to all intents and purposes has the same effect as avoiding the event in the first place. In other words, it is not what happens to us that matters but how we react to events that is the truly important thing.

A great deal has already been learned by both Eriu and the stranger, and this learning must inevitably change both of them in one way or another. This is really no more than the ordinary process of growing up which we all go through, and as we learn and experience so too do we change. It is important to realize that each individual must go through this process for him- or herself. Nobody can do it for another. This book, for example, can only ever give you an indication of how things might work through you, but until you actually experience the exercises given, and live by the principles described, you will never know whether or not they are right for you and suited to your temperament. All this is what the giving of the ring symbolizes.

To sum up, the male half, the warrior, has experienced and learned from mating with his female half, Eriu, and has recognized and understood the nature of the anxiety this mating has brought about. He realizes this to be a valuable experience (his gold ring), and that it cannot be imparted to anyone else (either by sale or by gift), it must be experienced and realized by everyone individually and personally. Eriu is told if she should meet anyone else who has recognized their own Polarity (someone whose finger it would fit) she will then be able to share their common experience and knowledge.

This can be seen happening in day-to-day life, where it has been noted that people who have shared a common or similar deep spiritual experience tend to gravitate towards one another even though they may rarely talk of their experience. They know there is no need for words or explanations; it is enough for each of them to know that what he or she experienced and gained from the experience is both personal and shared by others. This principle should be manifest in any worthwhile magical group where there is real power and knowledge, and can be used as a sort of test for any would-be new member or initiate to such a group. If the existing group members constantly talk of their work, and feel the need perpetually to explain and discuss what they have experienced, or think they have experienced, then that is probably about as far as they will ever get – merely talking about it. A good magician and magical group will probably appear, at least at first, as being very boring, and its members as having very little to say.

Section 20

Section 20 shows the need humans have to name and categorize things. Eriu has, so far, simply accepted all the above events, including the realization of her own Polarity. She is not sure, however, how to describe it all, or how to name the stranger. Her question 'I do not know who has come to me' also implies her concern for the future, in that she realizes she may need at some later stage to describe her experiences to others about to undergo similar experiences.

This can be seen as the birth of symbolism. What Eriu is asking for is a name, and names are no more than symbols for the objects to which they are attached. It is through symbolism we communicate, on all levels, and it is through mutually accepted symbolism that we can show others how to gain for themselves the progressive experiences we have had. Symbolism is also the link between the three levels of existence, and is therefore extremely important to the Irish system as a whole. Using a Biblical comparison again we can compare this to the section in the Book of Genesis where man gives names to all the animals.

Section 21

Section 21 contains quite a bit of information which will become relevant later, and also helps finish up the creation story which has been taking place on a personal level. The stranger, in answer to Eriu's question, identifies himself as Elatha mac Delbaith, king of the Fomoire. He is indeed from the Otherworld.

Elatha's father is Delbaith, king of the Fomoire; Eriu's father is Delbaeth, a king of the Tuatha De Danann. The similarity between these two names cannot be ignored, and it may well be that they are intended, in a symbolic way, to represent the same person, or at least two aspects of the same person. If this is the case then it would mean that Elatha and Eriu are brother and sister, and this would serve to strengthen the hidden symbolism of their actions in the discovery of each other's complementary, or Polar, half.

If, on the other hand, Delbaith and Delbaeth are intended to be two separate characters, as indeed the text implies (it may well be that Delba(i)eth is a title and not a personal name), then what has been described so far is a mating on an individual level of the Tuatha De Danann and the Fomoire. This has already happened earlier in the text when the two races united, resulting in the birth of Lug 'the glorious child'. As said earlier, the events being described from now on are of an individual, personal nature, but they should, nonetheless, reflect the previous macrocosmic events and happenings.

In reality either of these two explanations is acceptable, because the important point being put across is the necessity for the mental and spiritual aspects to join and integrate one with the other ultimately to produce a physical result or results. One translation of 'Delbaith' is in fact 'Fire Producer', and keeping in mind Fire's association with Gorias and the mental level, plus the obvious physical-level nature of the act of reproducing, this would seem to be covered in the text by giving these two characters' fathers the same title. This happened earlier when the three races of the Tuatha De Danann, the Fomoire and the Fir Bolg went through a conjoining process in order to produce the human race; now it is being repeated on a smaller scale by the predicted birth of Bres.

Eriu and Elatha have therefore successfully recognized and accepted their own opposite half or Polarity, have become aware of their own three levels of being and, in due course, will produce another physical being with the same component parts who will, hopefully, repeat this process of self-awareness, resulting in yet another being or beings. This is the fundamental pattern, which everything in the Green World, including human beings, follows. Simply stated, it is the desire and act of procreation.

Elatha makes a prediction concerning the expected child, and this means that his mental level is now aware of and using the spiritual level in order to make full use of his newly acquired intuitive powers. He tells Eriu that the child will be known as Eochu Bres and that he will become a standard by which beauty is measured. This ironically sets the scene for the first Irish satire (as we will see in Section 39), but for the moment Bres is exalted by his father, 'every beautiful thing that is seen in Ireland - both plain and fortress, ale and candle, woman and man and horse - will be judged in relation to that boy, so that people will then say of it, "It is a Bres."'

It is interesting to note that the beginning of Elatha's tribute reinforces Bres's link with the land (every beautiful thing that is seen in *Ireland*). This can be understood in two ways. First, Bres is destined to be king and is therefore inextricably linked with the land itself, his mother Eriu also being the spiritual aspect of the land, and second, he will become a perfected being who is conscious of, and works with, all three levels of his being, an act which can only ever be successful if carried out on the physical level. It can also be inferred from Elatha's description of Bres that he is not going to be an ordinary sort of king, who would more likely be described as mighty, wise, powerful, just, etc., rather than exceptionally beautiful.

It should be noted here that the name Bres does not occur in any other legend and, despite Elatha's assertion that it means beauty and will become a household name, there is no evidence of this word ever having been used in the context Elatha describes. This may be deliberate, because as subsequent events will reveal Bres was far from being the perfect king, and predicting his name would become an everyday word for beauty may be a bit of intentional irony.

Despite this, at the present stage everything indicates that he is going to be a very special being indeed. His mother is of the Tuatha De Danann and his father of the Fomoire, and he can be considered complementary to Lug, whose mother was of the Fomoire and whose father was of the Tuatha De Danann. Yet again the important concepts of Polarity and interchangeability are being explored, concepts which we first encountered in the opening sections of the legend concerning Findias and Murias. Both Lug and Bres are complete on all three levels, although presumably at this point Lug was still undergoing his instruction on Arran and had not yet manifested in the physical world. This double aspect of the kingship will be repeated, but on a lesser scale, later in the legend when Lug finally arrives at Tara and becomes king himself for a short while.

Section 22

Section 22 tells us that after the lovemaking, name-exchanging and the giving of the gold ring, each returns to their respective home and the 'famous conception' takes place. This stresses the point that an event as enormous as the realization of the complete nature of one's own self need only occur once. Each aspect returns to its own level, but takes with it the knowledge and awareness of the other.

It is important to note that the text tells us it was the conception which was given to Eriu at this stage and not the birth. This implies that such deep realizations must be pondered over for some time before becoming manifest in the physical world. It also, of course, means the following of the all-important laws of the Green World, in particular the need for a gestation period.

Also of significance, but easily missed, is the way that over the course of this whole important incident Elatha and Eriu are only specifically named once each. All other references to them are as either 'the man' or 'the woman'. This is a deliberate literary device used to show us that

the information being imparted in the narrative can apply
to any man or woman or, more precisely, to every man and
every woman, and should not be read as applying only to
some remote, 'fictional' characters.

Section 23

Section 23 concludes this passage with the birth of the boy
who is given the name his father decreed, Eochu Bres.
Elatha's predictions indicated that Bres would not be an
ordinary child, and this is seen by his rapid growth, twice
the rate of a normal child. Presumably, from the wording
of the text, this double-speed growing came to a halt after
seven years, which makes Bres fourteen years old. This age
is significant, as it was the age at which fosterage legally
ceased and the person was considered to be an
independent adult. Section 14 has already told us that Bres
was the adopted child of the Tuatha De Danann, so it was
probably at the age of fourteen he first took the throne.

This motif of rapid growth is not uncommon in these
ancient Irish texts, and simply serves to stress the
importance of the person being described and also
emphasizes the fact that he or she is consciously living
in both this world and the Otherworld at the same time –
hence the double passage of time. It could be argued, from
the events that follow, that Bres was immature and not yet
ready for kingship, but we should not fall into the trap of
reading these legends on a purely mundane level. The
events being described throughout the narrative are
disclosing principles that apply not just to the mundane,
ordinary world but to all three levels and to the
Otherworld as well. We should not limit our viewpoint
but strive to broaden it.

During the events that follow we should also bear in
mind that Bres is Lug's 'other half', or *Tanist* – a term still
used in the Irish parliamentary system – and because Lug
turns out to be the perfect king, Bres, by the very cosmic
principles we are investigating, must likewise turn out to
be the very opposite. This will become more obvious as
the story unfolds.

Practical Work: Exercise 3

A Journey to Findias

Your Inner Journey to the third city, Findias, follows exactly the same pattern as the previous two, with the following slight changes: the path on which your journey starts is very windy, with many leaves blowing about and a lot of dust; and, judging from the strength of the light, it is probably late afternoon. The little stream has become quite full again, and its surface is agitated by the wind. You can feel the small waves lapping against your legs as you wade across to the other side.

As you approach the city of Findias you notice that there are many windmills around it, its buildings have long, thin spires going high up into the sky, and on each spire is a great flag or banner fluttering noisily in the strong wind. When you enter the windy city itself the scene is much as in the other two cities, with busy streets and many people of all races and walks of life conversing and going about their business. One slight difference is that there seem to be more 'basic' sorts of buildings, such as shops, the butcher's, baker's, ironmonger's etc., and many business premises such as builders' yards, plumbers' and electricians' warehouses, and so on. In short, all the sort of trades and buildings you would expect to find in any town or city in Britain.

Your guide and friend appears as before and takes you through the blowy streets to a great tower right in the city centre. In the wooden doorway stands a mighty warrior grasping in his mailed hands a huge double-edged sword. He glares at you through the visor of his rough helmet and asks in a strong, demanding voice 'What are you doing in your own world to help and protect yourself?'

This question seems very strange and, as always, careful thought is needed before you give an answer. As you think about what the question actually implies a great deal is revealed about yourself as well as, hopefully, your own place and importance in this world.

Assuming that the warrior accepts your reply (and there is no guarantee he will unless you yourself are satisfied with it), you enter the tower and wend your way up the many stairs until the stairwell opens out onto a room at the top. Here sits Uiscias. He welcomes you openly to his place of study. Uiscias is much concerned with matters of personal learning and progress, and you can ask him whatever questions you like on these topics.

You need not stay in this Otherworld realm for long; once you have finished asking any questions that come to you for now, end the session by closing down as I have described in the earlier Practical Work. Be sure to write up your experiences in your Magical Diary and make yourself something to eat and drink.

During the days of your journeying to Findias you should also find time to look for a suitable sword to be used later in your magical Workings. Ideally a sword should be won, but nowadays having earned money by your own efforts with which to purchase one is just as acceptable. It should also be a real weapon capable of being used in self-defence, and not one of the cheap, fragile kinds sold nowadays by many 'occult' suppliers. Clearly it will take a bit of effort and hunting around to come up with a suitable weapon, but this is as much a part of the Practical Work as are the Inner Journeys and magical Workings which follow. If you cannot follow this simple discipline at this stage it is unlikely you will be able to apply the much greater discipline needed for the 'higher' aspects of this Work.

Chapter 5
Sections 24 - 32

From Section 24 onwards the narrative returns to where it in a sense left off at Section 14, and the events described from now on concern the long, slow learning process the Tuatha De Danann had to go through in this new, unfamiliar physical world. The experiences that they have and learn from are experiences that all of us can share and, likewise, learn from.

24. As a result of that contention which took place amongst the Tuatha De, the sovereignty of Ireland was given to that youth; and he gave seven guarantors from the warriors of Ireland (his maternal kinsmen) for his restitution of the sovereignty if his own misdeeds should give cause. Then his mother gave him land, and he had a fortress built on this land, Dun m Brese. And it was the Dagda who built that fortress.

25. But after Bres had assumed the sovereignty, three Fomorian kings (Indech mac De Domnann, Elatha mac Delbaith and Tethra) imposed their tribute upon Ireland - and there was not a smoke from a house in Ireland which was not under their tribute. In addition, the warriors of Ireland were reduced to serving him: Ogma beneath a bundle of firewood and the Dagda as a rampart builder, and he constructed the earthwork around Bres's fort.

26. Now the Dagda was unhappy at his work, and in the house he used to meet an idle, blind man named Cridenbel, whose mouth grew out of his chest.

Cridenbel considered his own meal small and the Dagda's large, so he said, 'Dagda, for the sake of your honour let the three best bits of your serving be given to me!' and the Dagda used to give them to him every night. But the satirist's bits were large: each bit was the size of a good pig. Furthermore those three bits were a third of the Dagda's serving. The Dagda's appearance was the worse for that.

27. Then one day the Dagda was in the trench and he saw the Mac Oc coming toward him.

'Greetings to you, Dagda!' said the Mac Oc.

'And to you,' said the Dagda.

'What makes you look so bad?' he asked.

'I have good cause,' he said, 'Every night Cridenbel the satirist demands from me the three best bits of my serving.'

28. 'I have advice for you,' said the Mac Oc. He puts his hand into his purse, and takes from it three coins of gold, and gives them to him.

29. 'Put,' he said, 'these three gold coins into the three bits for Cridenbel in the evening. Then these will be the best on your dish, and the gold will stick in his belly so that he will die of it; and Bres's judgement afterwards will not be right. Men will say to the king, "The Dagda has killed Cridenbel with a deadly herb which he gave him." Then the king will order you to be killed, and you will say to him, "What you say, king of the warriors of the Feni, is not a prince's truth. For he kept importuning me since I began my work, saying to me, 'Give me the three best bits of your serving, Dagda. My housekeeping is bad tonight.' Indeed, I would have died from that, had not the three gold coins which I found today helped me. I put them into my serving. Then I gave it to Cridenbel, because the gold was the best thing that was before me. So the gold is now in Cridenbel, and he died of it."

'It is clear,' said the king. 'Let the satirist's stomach be cut out to see whether the gold will be found in it. If it is not found, you will die. If it is found, however, you will live.'

30. Then they cut out the satirist's stomach to find the three gold coins in his belly, and the Dagda was saved.

31. Then the Dagda went to his work the next morning, and the Mac Oc came to see him and said, 'Soon you will finish your work, but do not seek payment until the cattle of Ireland are brought to you. Choose from among them the dark, black-maned, trained, spirited heifer.'

32. Then the Dagda brought his work to an end, and Bres asked him what he would take as wages for his labour. The Dagda answered, 'I require that you gather the cattle of Ireland in one place.' The king did that as he asked, and he chose the heifer from among them as the Mac Oc had told him. That seemed foolish to Bres. He had thought that he would have chosen something more.

Quite a lot takes place in these sections, but the overall themes are of the display of naïvety on Bres's part and the general learning process on the part of the Tuatha De Danann. The importance of sovereignty, the king's link with the land, the fact that this sovereignty is given to him by his people and is not an automatic right, and the matrilinear line of descent used by the Celts and their need to defend their honour at all costs are all emphasized here.

Bres's naïvety and his apparent inability to rule properly are hinted at in the way he is referred to in Section 24 as 'that youth'. He is clearly inexperienced at dealing with people; in the sections that follow we see he is easily manipulated by the Fomoire; he is tricked into a situation where he makes a false judgement – and worse, does not realize it; and he fails to realize that the Dagda's apparently ridiculous demand for the black heifer must mask some ulterior motive.

Section 24

Remember that at this stage in the legend Bres represents all of his people, and by analogy all of us today. Thus we can consider this passage as descriptive of the experiences most of us go through, and hopefully learn by, during adolescence. This is the age when we are very self-sure and tend to believe we know best, but it is also the age when we are most tricked, deceived and proved to be wrong time and time again by those who have passed us in the learning stakes.

The salutary lesson to learn from this passage is that it is very easy to get too confident mentally once we think we have mastered the physical level, but it is that very level upon which the others levels are based, at least while we are in a physical incarnation, and if we ignore or maltreat the physical level then it will surely turn against us. The physical level is powerful, and exerts its influence over the mental and spiritual. This is the cause of a vast number of diseases and maladies, a fact which modern psychiatry has finally acknowledged.

This situation is still to be seen among those who have given too much emphasis to their intellectual abilities, denying their other levels. There is the stereotypical 'absent-minded professor' who is so wrapped up in thought he shuffles about barely aware of his physical needs or appearance; or the cold, analytical scientist who explains everything away in terms of matter and energy and would never for one moment admit to the possibility of a spiritual realm because he or she cannot study and examine it. Today society is very much to blame for a great deal of this imbalance because of its overemphasis on gaining as many academic qualifications as possible. There is virtually no attention paid by the State to the physical well-being of its people, and no emphasis put on the spiritual well-being of the masses at all.

A couple of interesting points pertaining to Celtic society generally are highlighted in this section, namely the giving of guarantors or hostages and the need to defend personal honour at all costs. The giving and holding of hostages was a very common occurrence for a number of reasons. It usually happened when a new king took the throne, as in this case, and was in a sense a symbolic act rather than a means of persuasion or coercion. The hostages were always volunteers, were treated very well and held in high esteem and honour, and as such are not to be confused with the modern-day usage of the word, which implies persons held against their will in order to force a third party's hand. It should be noted that although Bres gave these seven guarantors to the Tuatha De Danann as a means of pledging his good intentions, even when he had made a mess of things, and imposed an unfair tax, the Tuatha De Danann did not revert to using his guarantors to force him to change. This would indicate that such hostages were symbolic as opposed to actual.

Section 25

The Dagda's association with the physical body and the physical earth are emphasized over and over again in this legend, and nearly every time he crops up in the text he is described as carrying out some physical function or other. In this section the functions are rampart- and ditch-building, but later on in the text they become much more personal, bodily functions. His name means 'The Good God' and, like most of the other deities, he has several other names, among them Eochaidh Ollathair, 'Father of All' and Ruad Rofhessa, 'Lord of Occult Knowledge'. Most sources agree that he is a master of the druidical arts. His father is none other than Elatha mac Delbaith, which means he is half-brother to Bres, and his children are Oengus Mac Oc, Aed Caem, Cermait Milbel and Brigit.

One of his brothers is Ogma, who is also mentioned in Section 25 as being put to hard graft by his half-brother Bres. The Dagda's and Ogma's father, Elatha mac Delbaith, is one of the Fomorian kings named in the same section as imposing a harsh tax on the Tuatha De Danann; one of the other Fomorian kings mentioned, Indech mac De Domnann, later kills Ogma in battle. Ogma was the great champion of the Tuatha De Danann, and whereas the Dagda represents the physical level generally, Ogma represents physical strength specifically.

The third Fomorian king alluded to, Tethra, is an obscure character and one we know little about, other than that he seems to have been associated with the sea, one of the poetic names for the waves of the sea being 'buar Tethrach', or 'cattle of Tethra'. It was said earlier that the obscure Tuatha De Dananns Fiacha and Edleo mac Allai could be contacted on an Inner level, and this applies likewise to Tethra – although, considering the unfavourable circumstances in which his name comes up in this passage, I would suggest that it might be better to leave him alone. Beings of the Otherworld can be just as nasty, unpleasant and deceitful as beings of this world.

Section 26

In this section we hear more of the Dagda. He is a very important character in this and other legends, and we have already been introduced to him earlier when we were told he was one of the custodians of the Four Treasures of the Tuatha De Danann, namely the cauldron. This cauldron, according to the earlier text, had the property that no one ever went away from it feeling unsatisfied. This seems a bit odd when we consider that according to the text the Dagda, the keeper of the cauldron, is slowly being starved to death. The answer to this apparent contradiction is twofold – the cauldron sustains on a spiritual level and not a physical one and, second, the Dagda in this passage represents the physical level slowly being destroyed by the unreasonable demands of the mental level, as represented by Bres's misrule and his alliance with the evil Fomoire. Cridenbel is another character who crops up a lot in the Irish legends, and again it may be the case that Cridenbel was a title rather than a personal name. He is always described as being a satirist. The Celts held satirists in great honour, which may have been partly out of fear, as it was believed that the worst possible thing that could happen to a man was to have satire levelled against him. It was believed that such an utterance would cause physical blotches to appear on a person's face and other frightful conditions to erupt spontaneously. It is for this reason that the Dagda gives in so easily to Cridenbel's unreasonable demands for food. This may also be a bit of contemporary comment, as it has been recorded that the satirists in ancient Ireland were eventually outlawed as they started to abuse their power totally and to make outrageous demands for no reason other than personal gain.

The repetition of the number three in this section is significant, and serves to indicate that the events being described have, or will have, repercussions on all three levels.

The name Cridenbel, if not a title, may mean something like 'his heart in his mouth' from the two words *cride* - heart, and *bel* - mouth. This would also make some sense of the curious description we are given of him: 'Cridenbel, whose mouth grew out of his chest'. The fact that he is described as being idle and blind would indicate a certain amount of contempt for him and, judging from his abuse of his position, this would be quite understandable. The terms idle and blind can also indicate his failure, or perhaps unwillingness, to operate fully on the mental and physical levels, an abusive situation in itself.

Section 27

The physical level can help us identify and point out errors made on the mental level by the use of those instincts and intuitions which we all have but usually ignore. This is what the Mac Oc represents and, as the Dagda learns, listening to his advice and following it through bring a solution to a previously unacceptable situation. This tells us that we should try hard to be aware of all three levels at all times, and to listen to what each may be trying to say. This should not be done only when things are going badly but also at those times when things appear to be going well and there are no immediate problems to deal with. Such times are in a sense the dangerous ones, when we become too confident and ignore the instincts and intuitions that may be trying to warn us of dangers just ahead.

The Mac Oc, which means 'young son', is the Dagda's own son, and this is a way of pointing out symbolically that he is in reality an aspect of the Dagda himself.

Section 28

Mac Oc, the Dagda's son, is a second-generation Tuatha De Danann, and as we saw in the case of Miach and Cian these children of the original inhabitants of this world seem to be more experienced and better equipped to cope and deal with the many problems and tribulations that constantly confront us. Mac Oc can be seen as representing the instinctive, intuitive part of our make-up, and it is he who appears with a solution just when all seems lost. His full name is Oengus Mac Oc, he is the son of the Dagda and the goddess Boand, who gave her name to the River Boyne, and although he is described as a god of love, and is credited with having had many love affairs, he does not appear to have left any offspring of his own. Although he is truly a great helper and lover of humanity, he is also a great trickster - and should consequently be handled with care.

Sections 29 - 32

The point made about the importance of personal honour is a theme that crops up time and time again in these Irish legends. Quite often the characters whose honour is challenged or insulted take things a bit too far, at least by modern standards, as in the case here, with the Dagda murdering Cridenbel simply so he no longer has to refuse the latter's requests for food, and thereby lose his honour. Generally speaking this defence of personal honour is a good thing, as it helps the individual have a healthy respect for his or her abilities and virtues, and is something we would do well to re-adopt as a society today - although I would suggest that the reader stops short of murder in defence of it!

It is clear that the members of the Tuatha De Danann are now taking on individual characteristics and attributes instead of being a collective race representative of humanity as a whole. By studying them, their personal characteristics and their relationships to each other, we can begin to see a great deal about our own personalities and our own place in society and this world as a whole - which is, after all, the important purpose of this book.

Practical Work: Exercise 4

A Journey to Murias

Your fourth and final Inner Journey to the cities takes you to Murias to meet Semias. Start in the usual manner, but note the following changes: the scene unfolds during a slight rain fall. The earth beneath your feet is wet and muddy and it looks as though night will soon be falling. The stream is in full spate and flowing hard and fast, and it takes quite an effort to wade through the strong current.

The wet roofs of Murias appear through the drizzle after a while, and you observe that there are many little rivers and streams flowing in and out of the city. The people and the buildings in Murias are very similar to those of Findias, although the streets are quieter due to the rain. Your guide appears and leads you off along the bank of one of the little rivers in the city until you eventually arrive at the site not of a building but of a great cave situated in the middle of what looks like some sort of public park surrounded by mature oak trees.

At the entrance to this cave stands a huge, rough, uncouth-looking creature who drinks sloppily and noisily from a great silver chalice which he grips with his two gnarled hands. When he sees you he stops drinking, wipes his lips on the back of his hairy wrist and demands of you in deep, guttural tones, 'What are you doing to protect and help the Green World of your place?'

His question, like the others before, makes you stop and think, and you feel very much 'on the spot', as if your reply will answer not only for you but for all of humanity as well. When you know how to reply, give him your answer with confidence and he will step aside and allow you to enter the great cavern.

Inside you find it is actually quite light and warm, and as you look back at the guardian of this place he seems to have taken on a much softer and far more pleasing appearance. In the centre of the cave sits Semias, who seems to be staring up at the roof as if trying to look into the very heart of the rock and soil above him. He turns to gaze at you and smiles when he recognizes you. Semias can tell you much about the workings of the Green World, the plant and animal kingdoms as well as the mineral kingdoms, and you can ask him anything you need to know on such matters.

As always, you should not deliberately try to stay in these Otherworld realms for longer than you really need to, so once your conversation has reached its natural conclusion, close down the session in the usual way and write up your Magical Diary before eating and drinking.

The Magical Weapon to be found during these days of visiting Murias and Semias is the cup. Ideally this should be given to you in true love and should be of the chalice type, preferably of silver. Do not worry too much if at first you feel you have little hope of obtaining any of the Magical Weapons as described, for by doing these Inner Journeys certain effects are being set up in the Otherworld, effects that will eventually manifest in this world, usually by apparently strange coincidences, whereby suddenly, out of the blue, the very things you are looking for will turn up just when you need them. This in itself is proof that things are going well, and is a confirmation that you are on the right track.

The rest of the Practical Work over the next ten chapters will concentrate on teaching you how to use these various Magical Weapons. You should continue, however, to explore the Four Cities, question the Four Teachers, and generally familiarize yourself with the landscape of the Otherworld as it appears to you.

Chapter 6
Sections 33 - 35

The next part of the legend deals with Nuadu and the fitting of his artificial arm, and looks further at how the Tuatha De Danann, both as a race and as individuals, are learning and coping in this world. The passage in question reads as follows:

33. Now Nuadu was being treated, and Dian Cecht put a silver hand on him which had the movement of any other hand. But his son Miach did not like that. He went to the hand and said, 'joint to joint of it, and sinew to sinew'; and he healed it in nine days and nights. The first three days he carried it against his side, and it became covered with skin. The second three days he carried it against his chest. The third three days he would cast white wisps of black bulrushes after they had been blackened in a fire.

34. Dian Cecht did not like that cure. He hurled a sword at the crown of his son's head and cut his skin to the flesh. The young man healed it by means of his skill. He struck him again and cut his flesh until he reached the bone. The young man healed it by the same means. He struck the third blow and reached the membrane of his brain. The young man healed this too by the same means. Then he struck the fourth blow and cut out the brain, so that Miach died; and Dian Cecht said that no physician could heal him of that blow.

35. After that, Miach was buried by Dian Cecht, and three hundred and sixty-five herbs grew through the grave,

corresponding to the number of his joints and sinews. Then Airmed spread her cloak and uprooted those herbs according to their properties. Dian Cecht came to her and mixed the herbs, so that no one knows their proper healing qualities unless the Holy Spirit taught them afterwards. And Dian Cecht said, 'Though Miach no longer lives, Airmed shall remain.'

Once again a good deal of information is imparted and yet more characters are introduced. The main theme of this passage is a warning about the negative and very destructive effects of the emotion of jealousy. The jealousy in this case is expressed by Dian Cecht against his own son Miach, who effects a better repair to Nuadu's hand than he himself was capable of. This jealousy is, in a sense, the negative side of the protection of personal honour which we examined in Chapter 5. Dian Cecht feels his own honour and prestige have been lessened somewhat by the fact that his son managed to do a better job than he did, and he expresses this slight to his honour in a very jealous and aggressive way.

Section 33

The wording of Section 33 implies that Miach did not give Nuadu back his own hand, although other versions of this same story say he did. In this version however Miach makes flesh and blood grow onto the silver hand – 'He went to the hand . . . and it became covered with skin.' This in effect means he improved on the work which his father had already initiated. The message behind this could be that while there is always room for improvement, be careful you don't upset anybody in the process!

The nine days taken to effect the cure are clearly magical, and the last three days are particularly interesting in that we come across the very curious theme of casting wisps at someone. This theme crops up in other Irish legends, although the effect of such druidical actions in these other tales is invariably to drive the person concerned mad.

One example concerns Nuadu Fullon (perhaps it is no coincidence his first name is the same), an early king of

Leinster who was named 'Fullon' after his druidical teacher of that name. This druid is credited as being the first to use the magical wisp of straw, called 'Dlui Fulla' or 'Fluttering Wisp', the effect of which was to drive people mad. Simply by throwing the wisp in their face they were made to run, jump or flutter about like lunatics. It is therefore interesting to note that this same procedure is used here, and on a character with the same name (rather than being used by him as in the other tale), with the overall effect in this instance being beneficial rather than harmful. The use of the Dlui Fulla would seem to have been widely known, but is, sadly, yet another piece of Irish Celtic magic which we have lost.

The two new characters introduced here are the brother and sister Miach and Airmed, two of the children of Dian Cecht. Dian Cecht was the great physician of the Tuatha De Danann, although in this passage he is clearly outshone by his son, and he in turn is outshone by his sister. This serves to emphasize what has already been noted about the greater skills and abilities of second-generation Tuatha De Danann. On this same topic we could note here that the 'glorious child' Lug is Dian Cecht's grandson, and therefore a third-generation Tuatha De Danann – and, as we shall see, the most skilled of them all.

The Dian Cecht/Miach relationship is the third father/son relationship to appear so far in this legend. The first was Elatha and Bres, the second the Dagda and Mac Oc. Each of these relationships has been very different. This is only to be expected when we remember that these various characters are intended to represent every facet and feature of the human race as we know it today. The acts which each carries out, and the way in which the others react to them, are the truly instructive parts of this legend, and are the parts that merit our greatest attention.

Section 34

The fact that Dian Cecht uses a sword with which to murder Miach is of significance. It was noted at the beginning of the legend that Nuadu is closely associated with the sword in an archetypal way. Here we learn that Miach heals Nuadu (and presumably now makes him once more eligible for the kingship), yet the result of this is that he dies by Nuadu's own weapon. This association between Nuadu, the sword, a negative emotion and a subsequent death is, in motif, identical to the circumstances described in the passage concerning the Dagda and his treatment and actions. There we saw the Dagda, who is associated with the cauldron, a negative emotion (Cridenbel's distorted use of his position), and a subsequent death. The association of deities with various weapons and articles is clearly very important, and requires a good deal of study if we are to understand it and get the most from it.

The important message of this short passage is therefore that we must guard against the very destructive properties of the negative emotion of jealousy. The repetition of the numbers three and nine used throughout this passage underline its significance.

Section 35

Section 35 is one of the few in the legend where we can positively identify some sort of tampering, or more accurately the insertion of text, on the part of the scribes who set the story down in writing. The sentence '. . . no one knows their proper healing qualities unless the Holy Spirit taught them afterwards' is obviously a Christian-era embellishment, although it must be noted that it in no way changes the sense or meaning of the original text and, if anything, it illustrates the organic nature of the legend, as it adapts well to this intrusion, and offers us an example of the scribes' attempts to 'bring it up to date' by giving it a relatively modern Christian context.

The part dealing with the healing herbs growing from Miach's grave is symbolic of the fact that knowledge can be passed on from person to person even after physical death. It also implies that there is a cure for each and every illness. The number of herbs mentioned, 365, represents one for each day of the year and, by implication, one for the whole of time and everything and anything that can happen during the passage of time.

Airmed shows a very keen foresight by realizing the importance of these herbs and by spreading them out on her cloak in their correct order and positions. Unfortunately Dian Cecht's uncontrollable jealousy once again gets the better of him, and he so upsets the crucial order of the life-giving plants that we are still trying to sort out the tangle today. Luckily for Airmed his jealousy stops short of murdering her!

Any reader interested in herb-lore or healing generally should realize from this passage that any Inner Work carried out with Airmed should prove very fruitful, and serious Work along these lines is to be encouraged. The exercises contained in this book should help you learn the skills you need in order to carry out such serious Inner Work, and hopefully, if enough people apply themselves to it, we shall one day see Airmed's cloak spread out with the 365 herbs once more in their proper place. There is a lot of very powerful imagery here, it would be a shame to ignore its message.

Practical Work: Exercise 5

Preparing Your Magical Weapons

Now that you have collected your four Magical Weapons, and before you start to use them, it is necessary to consecrate and cleanse them of any unwanted influences that may be stuck to them. The principle behind this is exactly the same as in cleaning and sterilizing surgical instruments prior to an operation - the removal of any contamination or infection that may jeopardize the operation in hand.

Because your Magical Weapons are going to be the tools with which you learn to understand and manipulate the Elemental powers of this world and their Otherworld aspects, it is vital to make sure that the tools being used are clean (in all senses of the word) and dedicated solely for your purposes. You cannot use your magical sword for splitting firewood and then expect to be able to use it to its full potential in a magical ritual shortly afterwards, any more than you would use a surgical scalpel to peel potatoes and then expect to be able to use it for an appendectomy!

Your Magical Weapons must be treated with respect and care; your mental attitude towards them is as important as the way in which you handle and use them physically. If both of these are done correctly, then the Weapons' own inherent spiritual aspect will start to make itself felt within you.

To cleanse and consecrate your Weapons you must first find an open place - preferably a wild area of forest or moorland, for example, which has not been shaped by humanity, although a secluded garden would do if needs must - where you can work for a night and a day without being disturbed and where you have access to both soft earth and running water. This place should be chosen with care; you will use it many times for both ritual work and also for personal meditative or Inner Journey workings. Finding such a place is also a good way of making yourself look closely at the environment immediately around you, and should help to get you started on the path to becoming closer to the Green World. This in itself is a very important part of the Irish Magical Tradition.

Once you have found your working area, go there with your Weapons and something with which to dig a small hole in the earth. This should be done at dusk and, ideally, at either Beltaine (1st May) or Samhain (31st October) although this is not vital and, indeed, may not be practical. Spend a few moments when you get there stilling your thoughts and body and generally tuning in to the feel of the place. Listen for the birdsong; is there a wind or breeze? How does the sky look? Did you pass any animals, wild or domesticated, on the way there?

Keeping in mind the task in hand, that is, the dedicating and cleansing of your Magical Weapons, dig a hole wide enough to place your stone, wand, sword and cup into. It does not have to be very deep so long as all the Weapons are completely covered once you have filled it back in. Leave them in the earth overnight; you can spend the night out in your wild place with your Weapons if you wish; if you don't you should be there for dawn the following day. Overnight try to see in your mind's eye the slow, steady powers of the Element of Earth working their way into the Weapons and, at the same time, forcing out anything already there which is unwanted or unclean. Such unwanted and unclean parts are absorbed by the surrounding earth and broken down in order for their component parts to be reassembled into something constructive and useful. This is one of the dynamic laws of the Green World and, consider, will apply to your own physical body one day.

At dawn the next day you should dig up your Weapons carefully and take them to your place of running water. Place all four Weapons in the water in such a way that the flow runs along the length of the wand and the sword and flows into the mouth of your cup. The stone can lie flat on the bed of the stream or river. Again, as they lie in the physical water, be aware of the power of the Element of Water flowing into and through them and, likewise, driving out that which is unclean and unnecessary. See these aspects flowing out of each Weapon and being carried off and diluted by the flowing, living water.

Leaving your Weapons in the water, you should build a small fire. This fire should ideally be made from as many of the different types of wood that surround your sacred place as you can find, but if this is impractical it should nonetheless be made from fallen wood which you have gathered yourself. The Weapons should be left in the water until midday, when they should be taken out and carefully passed through the flames of the little fire. As before, as you carefully pass each Weapon one by one through the flames and smoke, see the unwanted parts being burnt up and dissolving into the air with the fire smoke and the Weapon itself being charged with the very essence of Elemental Fire and all it symbolizes. Do this for as long as the fire burns, taking care all the time not to accidentally burn or damage your Weapons. Do however stop once dusk starts to settle in.

At dusk you should suspend your Magical Weapons in the evening air, either by hanging them from a bush or tree or, at a push, by holding them aloft yourself. As the air blows around them visualize it blowing through them and, as before, pushing out the unwanted, unclean parts of the Weapons and replacing them with the spirit of the Element of Air. The Weapons should be left suspended until darkness falls.

Once it is dark take your Weapons and return home. Put them carefully in the special place you have reserved for them and do not handle them again until you are ready to perform the little ritual set out in Chapter 13.

Now, after a night and a day, your Magical Weapons have been cleansed and charged and are ready for you to use, and to be stamped with your own individuality, for they are, after all, extensions of yourself.

While undertaking this Practical Work in your special place, spend time fruitfully by observing the goings-on of the Green World around you more rigorously than you have ever done before. Be aware of the pulsating life-force that courses through everything, animate and (apparently) inanimate; try to feel at one with that flow. Always do this whenever you are in the Green World. Remember that you are an integral part of it and not just an observer who happens to be passing through a particular place at a particular time.

If the above procedure proves to be genuinely impossible for you to carry out then it is perfectly adaptable to being moved indoors. As with any magical and ritual work it is the intention that is important and not just the physical actions or where those actions are carried out. Do try hard though to find a suitable Green World location – it will all feel so much better.

Chapter 7
Sections 36 - 39

Our examination of the main text now continues with
Sections 36 to 39:

36. At that time, Bres held the sovereignty as it had been
granted to him. There was great murmuring against
him among his maternal kinsmen the Tuatha De, for
their knives were not greased by him. However
frequently they might come, their breaths did not
smell of ale; and they did not see their poets nor their
bards nor their satirists nor their harpers nor their
pipers nor their horn-blowers nor their jugglers nor
their fools entertaining them in the household. They
did not go to contests of those pre-eminent in the arts,
nor did they see their warriors proving their skill at
arms before the king, except for one man, Ogma the
son of Etain.
37. This was the duty which he had, to bring firewood to
the fortress. He would bring a bundle every day from
the islands of Clew Bay. The sea would carry off two-
thirds of his bundle because he was weak for lack of
food. He used to bring back only one third, and he
supplied the host from day to day.
38. But neither service nor payment from the tribes
continued; and the treasures of the tribe were not
being given by the act of the whole tribe.
39. On one occasion the poet came to the house of Bres
seeking hospitality (that is, Coirpre son of Etain, the
poet of the Tuatha De). He entered a narrow, black,

dark little house; and there was neither fire nor furniture nor bedding in it. Three small cakes were brought to him on a little dish - and they were dry. The next day he arose, and he was not thankful. As he went across the yard he said,

'Without food quickly on a dish,
Without cow's milk on which a calf grows,
Without a man's habitation after darkness remains,
Without paying a company of storytellers - let that be Bres's condition.'

'Bres's prosperity no longer exists,' he said, and that was true. There was only blight on him from that hour; and that is the first satire that was made in Ireland

Quite a bit of information relating to ancient Celtic society is given in this passage, and certain qualities are displayed which we would do well to consider reintroducing into our own, present-day society. Another new character, Coirpre son of Etain, is introduced, and Bres makes yet another disastrous blunder.

Section 36

The text makes it clear that hospitality was the priority of the day, and that to be inhospitable, stingy or mean, especially while trying to maintain a pretence of hospitality, was considered to be the greatest fault in a person's character and one that would certainly not go unnoticed or without comment. It is also clear from the text that the concept of hospitality included not only the obvious requirements of providing a guest with food, warmth and shelter, but also with entertainment and various pleasurable pursuits. In today's world, to offer free hospitality, where practical, is certainly a trait that would not go amiss, and in a similar manner the pursuit of pleasure for pleasure's sake is something to be encouraged. For some odd reason our society encourages feelings of guilt for enjoying things for their own sake - this is not a healthy sign. It should be noted that all the pleasures described are of such a type that everyone can partake of them, and at the same time none of them cause any pain, discomfort, degradation or embarrassment to those providing the entertainment. Would that were true of many of our so-called entertainments today.

Section 37

The treatment meted out by Bres to Ogma is almost identical to that experienced by his brother the Dagda at the hands of Cridenbel in Section 26. Clearly Bres has failed to learn anything from the incident involving the Dagda, Mac Oc and Cridenbel. The Dagda was forced to give up two-thirds of his food, which is fuel for the body, while in this case Ogma loses two-thirds of the firewood, or fuel for the hearth. As noted earlier, when the number three or its multiples occurs in the text we know we are reading something of greater import than its surface meaning might indicate.

As a general rule of thumb we could say that when the numbers are whole numbers – 3, 6, 9, 27 and so on – the meaning to be looked for in the text is a positive one; but when we are dealing in fractions – a third, two-thirds, etc., as we have here – then the implied meaning is a negative one.

The underlying theme to these incidents is that a reversal of the normal order of things has occurred. Two of the great gods of the Tuatha De Danann have been reduced to servile roles and are treated very badly, and Bres, the High King, is making stupid decisions and generally making a total mess of his rulership despite the fantastic prophecies made prior to his birth. To cap it all, the poet Coirpre makes a satire against Bres (and by implication against the land and all of his people), and that is more damaging than an all-out attack by the fiercest of opponents in battle.

There is also an association between gathering firewood and madness, which can be gleaned from other texts, the full significance of which has been lost to us today. The point behind Ogma being described as a wood-gatherer is that due to Bres's inability to rule effectively the normal order of things has been completely upset, to such an extent that the great champion of the Tuatha De Danann has been driven mad and spends his day floundering about in the sea chasing after lost firewood.

Section 38

Section 38 starts to give us an indication that the ordinary people are unhappy with Bres's rulership and are considering taking matters into their own hands. Considering that Bres represents every one of us, including you the reader, we can read into this that our own actions will inevitably affect not only those directly involved but, eventually, everyone else in one way or another. If our motives are not favourable then we shall soon become victims of our own bad or inept actions. Modern-day scientists, especially those involved in ecological studies, are beginning to realize this vital fact, and are warning that you cannot tackle a problem in isolation but must consider the planet, and all that it contains, as a whole. I would extend this to include a consideration of the beings and contents of the Otherworld as well. I wonder when science will eventually catch on to this important point.

Section 39

The new character introduced in this passage is Coirpre son of Etain, poet of the Tuatha De Danann and either brother or half-brother to Bres, the Dagda and Ogma. His first name, Coirpre, is probably a corruption of some similar-sounding name, because the inclusion of the letter 'p' in his name is foreign, not originally being part of the Irish alphabet. This distinction leads me to describe the classification of the ancient Celts into *P-Celts* and *Q-Celts*. The P-Celts were, broadly speaking, the Welsh and British, who had the 'p' sound in their language. The Q-Celts were the Irish and Scottish, who did not have the 'p' sound but utilized a hard 'q' sound in its place – for example, the word for 'son of' in Welsh was *map* and in Irish *maq*, or *mac*. This can be a useful rule of thumb when studying Irish legends – if a character has a name or title that includes the letter 'p', then either the original name has been corrupted or he or she is a character borrowed from another tradition not originally Irish.

The events surrounding Coirpre are similar to those in the passage studied in Chapter 5, which dealt with the satirist Cridenbel. The main difference is that Cridenbel was disliked and came off badly in his confrontation, whereas Coirpre is respected by his people and most definitely comes out on top. The fact that Coirpre is related in one way or another to each of the main characters described so far – unlike Cridenbel who was a comparative stranger – helps to maintain a link or continuous thread throughout these seemingly unrelated incidents, and this in turn helps to keep a continuous line of instruction flowing.

The main event being described in this passage is Coirpre's poor treatment by Bres and his subsequent satire against him. As said earlier, hospitality was of the utmost importance, and for a king to treat such a respected member of the community in such a shameful manner was unheard of. This of course is a reflection upon the state of the whole of the Tuatha De Danann, which Bres represents, and Coirpre's satire is therefore directed not just against the king but all of the people as well. This is implied by the fact that he uttered the satire 'As he went across the yard . . .' and not directly to Bres himself. In other words it was directed at Bres's household, and therefore everybody, and not just against Bres personally.

It is interesting to note that under the Brehon Laws, generally acknowledged as being the oldest surviving legal system in Europe and covering every conceivable aspect of civil and criminal law, a king who tolerated a satire was listed among the seven types who were not entitled to honour price, i.e. compensation for wrong done against one, which rose in value in accordance with the status (or honour) of the individual. Kings normally were due the highest honour price, but as mentioned here no king was entitled to an honour price, no matter how badly he had been wronged, if he tolerated a satire.

The Celts believed that the power of satire was utterly devastating, but Coirpre's final statement, 'Bres's prosperity no longer exists' is no more than a confirmation of the situation as it stood prior to his satire. This belief in the power of satire may not be as superstitious as it may at first appear. If we replace the word satire with, say, libel, slander, mockery or even sarcasm, and consider these in a modern context and the very damaging effect each can have on our reputation and livelihood, then we can begin to realize the destructive power of satire to the ancient Celts. The modern proverb 'the pen is mightier than the sword' exemplifies this belief in the power of the word, written or spoken, and we have already been shown how much damage swords can inflict – how much more then can words inflict?

This power of satire is one that each of us today can still wield, and it is one that some people use very skilfully indeed, although more often than not they use it for no other reason than spitefulness or personal satisfaction. It should be noted that Coirpre is described as a poet and not a satirist. The only satirist named in the legend is Cridenbel, and his power of satire, or rather the threat of it as he never actually used it, did him no good at all and in fact was the cause of his eventual death. Coirpre, who did use his power of satire with devastating effects, is a poet, and we know that Celtic poets underwent very long and arduous training before they earned the title. Part of this training was instruction in when and when not to use the great power they wielded. This should remind us of the need to exercise caution today should we ever consider using our own in-built powers of satire. Of course this warning also applies generally to any of our powers and on any level.

Practical Work: Exercise 6

Preparing Your Working Area

The first five exercises have introduced you to the Four Teachers of the Tuatha De Danann, tested your resourcefulness and initiative in finding suitable Magical Weapons, and shown you how to purify and charge your Weapons while at the same time testing your resolve to find a suitable Green World location in which to work and, once there, expecting you to study closely and to learn from all that was going on around you.

The next step is to prepare your working area on both an Inner and an Outer level for regular use. Just as it was necessary to purify and make ready your Magical Weapons, so too is it necessary to purify and prepare the area in which those Weapons will be used.

Once again this is a matter of magical hygiene, and is as important to the magician as sterilizing the operating theatre before an operation is to a surgeon.

Your working area should be big enough for you to be able to move at least nine feet around in all directions, although ideally it should be even larger than this if possible. If outdoors it should be in a flat area with no immediate obstructions such as bushes, plants or protruding rocks or boulders and, preferably, sheltered on all sides by trees or some similar natural screen. Clearly it will not be easy to find such an ideal place, but the benefit of putting such restrictions and conditions on your site is that it may force the more naturally lazy among us to get up and physically go into the Green World and hunt around. Those who are not prepared to make this little effort will never venture far with their magical endeavours, either, and in short would be advised to put this book down at this stage and take up some sedentary hobby with no accompanying physical, mental or spiritual effort.

If finding a Green World location is simply impossible, either because of a physical disability that makes journeys to the Green World impossible, or due to the demands of your home-life or restrictions of your home's location, then it is perfectly feasible to use a suitable room in your own home. The powers of the Otherworld are not really very interested in the immediate physical surroundings of the working magician, and will respond just as well to a request made from your living-room as they will to one made deep in the heart of an oak grove. The finding and using of an open-air site is for the benefit of the magician and no other – but that benefit, in itself, is great.

To prepare your area for working you must clearly define in your mind's eye the exact area in which you intend to move around and complete your various magical rituals, Inner Journeys, etc. This area should be circular and should be of sufficient diameter to enable you to take several paces in all directions from the centre.

Work out which direction is North, then take up your stone and go to the northernmost point of the circumference of your circle and start to walk clockwise, i.e. following the natural direction of the sun's movement, around the circumference of your circle, all the while holding your stone in both hands in front of you. By doing this you are physically defining the limits of the circle's existence. Walk three times round this circumference, one circumambulation for each of the three levels. While doing this constantly be aware of the purpose behind it. Visualize the area being cleansed, on all three levels, of all unnecessary and unwanted attributes that may be lurking there unseen. Repeat the above process with your wand, sword, and cup, concentrating all the time on the cleaning and purifying aspects of the work in hand.

Once these twelve circumambulations have been completed, take your sword, go to the northern quarter again, and describe on the ground, in a clockwise direction, the circumference of the circle using the point of your sword. When this has been completed return to the centre of the circle and place your Magical Weapons on the ground. As you stand there realize that you are the centre of the circle, that the circle has no existence beyond the limits which you have described, that the cutting edge of the sword has cut a divide between the two worlds and that you are now the centre of both of these realms of existence – and that, literally, the whole Universe is rotating around you as its centre.

The circle can be considered in its three-dimensional aspect as coming to a point some distance above your head, and thus forming a cone shape. Likewise it extends down into the ground in a similar cone shape, and thereby totally encapsulates you within it. If you wish, at this point you can spend a few moments seated on the ground, meditating over the significance of what you have just done and trying to clarify in your mind the massive amount of symbolism attached to the circle and cone shapes.

When you are ready to close the working, take your sword and go again to the northern quarter. Once again trace the circumference of your circle, but this time move

in an anti-clockwise direction. Be aware of the gap
between the two worlds being re-sealed and closed off once
more. When you return to the northern quarter,
circumambulate three times in an anti-clockwise
direction (there is no need to take each Weapon with you
this time), consciously closing down the magical aspect
of each of the three levels with each circumambulation.
Take up your Weapons and return quietly and calmly to
your home, or, if you're already there, leave the room and
go to another part of the house in order to give you time
to shut off your magical associations with that room and
replace them with your normal day-to-day associations
with it.

Finally, as always, write up your notes in your Magical
Diary and have a drink and something to eat.

Chapter 8
Sections 40 - 51

The next block to be examined, Sections 40 to 51, deals with the actions of the ordinary people to depose their unsuitable king, and his reactions to their efforts:

40. Now after that the Tuatha De went together to talk with their adopted son Bres mac Elathan, and they asked him for their sureties. He gave them restoration of the kingship, and they did not regard him as properly qualified to rule from that time on. He asked to remain for seven years. 'You will have that,' the same assembly agreed, 'provided that the safeguarding of every payment that has been assigned to you - including house and land, gold and silver, cattle and food - is supported by the same securities, and that we have freedom of tribute and payment until then.' 'You will have what you ask,' Bres said.

41. This is why they were asked for the delay: that he might gather the warriors of the sid, the Fomoire, to take possession of the Tuatha by force provided he might gain an overwhelming advantage. He was unwilling to be driven from the kingship.

42. Then he went to his mother and asked her where his family was. 'I am certain about that,' she said, and went unto the hill from which she had seen the silver vessel on the sea. She then went onto the shore. His mother gave him the ring which had been left with her, and he put it around his middle finger, and it fitted him. She had not given it up for anyone, either by sale or gift.

Until that day, there was none of them whom it would
fit.

43. Then they went forward until they reached the land of
the Fomoire. They came to a great plain with many
assemblies upon it, and they reached the finest of
these assemblies. Inside, people sought information
from them. They answered that they were of the men
of Ireland. Then they were asked whether they had
dogs, for at that time it was the custom, when a group
of men visited another assembly, to challenge them to
a friendly contest. 'We have dogs,' said Bres. Then the
dogs raced, and those of the Tuatha De were faster than
those of the Fomoire. Then they were asked whether
they had horses to race. They answered, 'We have,' and
they were faster than the horses of the Fomoire.

44. Then they were asked whether they had anyone who
was good at sword-play, and no one was found among
them except Bres. But when he lifted the hand with the
sword, his father recognized the ring on his finger and
asked who the warrior was. His mother answered on
his behalf and told the king that Bres was his son.She
related to him the whole story as we have recounted it.

45. His father was sad about him, and asked, 'What force
brought you out of the land you ruled?'

Bres answered, 'Nothing brought me except my own
injustice and arrogance. I deprived them of their
valuables and possessions and their own food. Neither
tribute nor payment was ever taken from them until
now.'

46. 'That is bad,' said his father. 'Better their prosperity
than their kingship. Better their requests than their
curses. Why then have you come?' asked his father.

47. 'I have come to ask you for warriors,' he said, 'I intend
to take that land by force.'

48. 'You ought not to gain it by injustice if you do not gain
it by justice,' he said.

49. 'I have a question then: what advice do you have for
me?' said Bres.

50. After that he sent him to the champion Balor,
grandson of Net, the king of the Hebrides, and to
Indech mac De Domnann, the king of the Fomoire;
and these gathered all the forces from Lochlainn

westwards to Ireland, to impose their tribute and their rule upon them by force, and they made a single bridge of ships from the Hebrides to Ireland.

51. No host ever came to Ireland which was more terrifying or dreadful than that host of the Fomoire. There was rivalry between the men from Scythia of Lochlainn and the men out of the Hebrides concerning that expedition.

Section 40

The principle that a king is allowed to rule only for as long as his people wish him to is demonstrated in Section 40, where we read that the Tuatha De Danann felt it necessary to go to Bres and discuss his leadership with him face to face. The relationship between the king and his subjects was more akin to the relationship that exists today between a Member of Parliament and his or her constituents than to the relationship between the present monarch and her subjects.

The fact that Bres does listen to them and comes to an agreement with them rather than simply refusing to see them shows that he realizes his tentative position and feels compelled to comply, at least on the surface, with the will of the people. The situation for the Tuatha De Danann is clearly bad and getting worse all the time, and it is therefore curious to read that they so readily agree to give him another chance and let him rule for a further seven years, with only the usual sureties and bonds for his kingship. The reason for this may be that no other suitable candidate exists (it is not clear from the text whether all this was taking place before, during or after the restoration of Nuadu's amputated hand), or it may be because Bres gives his word that he will improve and that things will change.

To the Celts a man's word was his honour. It has already been demonstrated clearly by events thus far just how important personal honour was deemed. If someone gave his or her word on a subject, then there was an end to it; it need not be questioned again. It was unthinkable that people would ever go back on their word or not do their utmost to fulfil that which they had promised. Since Bres promises to change and make a go of things then no other sureties or bonds are asked for, and the people agree to a fair trial period during which to reassess his progress.

This giving of one's word and sticking to it no matter the cost is a virtue we have clearly lost today, to the extent that, like it or not, we do not trust one another and, as a species, humanity cannot be trusted at all. Rediscovering the importance of honesty and the giving of one's word is something that surely deserves serious consideration and strenuous attempts. To be realistic, there is very little likelihood of the whole human race readopting this stance, but there is no reason why as individuals we cannot reintroduce this tenet into our own daily lives.

Even the effort is likely to meet with suspicion initially, for no other reason than people are not used to complete and open honesty and trustworthiness. But persist, for wouldn't it be a great achievement for one to be accepted without question as a man or woman who could be trusted, who is known always to stick by one's word and likewise to accept the word of others? It should be understood, though, that adopting this attitude is no easy matter. It is a sure way of revealing just how deceitful and untruthful we really are. Try it for, say, a period as short as one week. It is extremely difficult to do, and quite a salutary experience. It can also cost friendships and jobs! This indicates just how far we have drifted from this simple and basic attribute.

The trial term of office given by the people to Bres, i.e. seven years, may be symbolic and not necessarily seven actual solar years. This same period crops up time and time again throughout the Irish legends, and would seem to represent no more than a reasonable period in which to allow ample time for events to occur or for people to change. There is a very great deal of symbolism attached to the number seven, but I would suggest that none of it applies here. At times it is too easy, while examining these legends for 'hidden meanings', to ascribe anything and everything with masses of symbolism and ignore the fact that perhaps a specific or detail given is in reality very simple and straightforward. The meaning then of the seven years is no more than it represents a reasonable amount of time for Bres to sort himself out as a person and as a ruler.

This concept of an 'ideal' period of time is perhaps reflected in the Brehon Laws, which seem not to legislate for society as it actually was but for how society *should* have been, in an ideal situation. It is true that there were hundreds of laws and statutes that were indeed applied and invoked when necessary, but there are even more that dealt with such intricate, complicated and highly unlikely situations that they can be read as no more than exercises in what could or should happen if society ever achieved perfection. This, to my mind, shows a very high degree of forethought and intelligence on the part of the ancient Celts.

Section 41

Section 41, unfortunately, brings us back to reality with a nasty jolt, for it is clear that all the time the Tuatha De Danann and Bres were negotiating his new lease of life, he was harbouring thoughts of fleeing to the Fomoire and seeking the help he would need to rule his people by force. Bres, in other words, is a liar. It is perhaps worth noting here that nowhere in the legend is it recorded that Bres underwent the trial of the Stone of Fal before being given his kingship. If he had he would surely never have passed, but the fact that this vital test was omitted only serves to reflect the imperfect state the Tuatha De Danann were in at that time, a state which has contributed so greatly to their present predicament.

What this means in Bres's case is that his rulership has got so bad, and his ego so inflated, that he is contemplating desperate measures to cling to his kingship, for no other reason than his own satisfaction and lust for power. On a personal level (remember that whatever we can say of Bres we can say of the individual) this section can be read as a salutary warning that this same situation can crop up in our own day-to-day lives; we must be ever vigilant against it and recognize what to do should it happen. It is probably most notable and easily recognized in the leaders of magical groups, who, if not very careful, can develop inflated egos and become nothing short of tyrants, expecting their poor group members to obey without question their every whim. It can happen in any group situation where one person is recognized as being the leader, and therefore anybody in such a leadership position must constantly be aware of the dangers the post carries with it, and must be ever self-watchful. Leaders of magical groups, however, are especially prone to this very real danger due to the nature of the powers they are dealing with.

It is interesting to note from Section 41 that Bres is described as leaving to 'gather the warriors of the sid, the Fomoire', since it is usually put forward by Celtic scholars that the Sid (pronounced 'shee') were in fact the remnants of the Tuatha De Danann who at quite a late date were forced underground (underground being the original meaning of the word 'sid'), and who took on the nature of fairies or Nature spirits. Here in the text, however, the Tuatha De Danann are very much the ruling race, and have not yet been forced underground or anywhere else for that matter. The wording specifically implies that the Sid were considered to be the Fomoire and clearly not the Tuatha De Danann. If this is so, it puts a very different light on just who the Sid were and what they were like. Fortunately we do not need to bother ourselves with whether the Sid were originally the Fomoire, the legend about whom got confused over time; the sense of the text is clear – Bres fled to the Fomoire for help in taking Ireland by force.

Section 42

Section 42, on the surface, appears straightforward enough. Bres asks his mother how he can get in touch with his father. The inner meanings of this section, however, are much deeper and very important; and, in essence, this passage could be described as a magical ritual or formula.

The first event described is that of Bres going to his mother for some specific piece of information. Keeping in mind that these characters represent various aspects of ourselves and the world around and within us, we could put this another way: The magician, or seeker, has to go to the source of Knowledge, which in this case is Ireland or the Earth itself, in order to gain previously unknown information.

Bres's mother's reaction is to rise to a higher state, as she already did in Section 16. This time presumably she takes Bres with her. She then gives him his father's ring, which is symbolic of putting him in touch with his father, who represents even higher and more powerful forces. All this is described as happening on a shore – as we noted earlier, shores are very significant places due to their 'in-between' nature. All of this combines to put them into a state where very powerful magic can be worked.

The last two sentences of Section 42 imply that up until then nobody else had used, or perhaps was able to use, such powerful magical forces. This may imply that the keeper of the ring, the power, who was Eriu or Ireland, chose not to give it to anyone else who had asked for it. This illustrates an important magical point, which can be summed up in the following way: we all have free will which we use to govern our actions in this world, both magical and otherwise. It should be understood, however, that the Earth too has free will, as do all the inhabitants of the Otherworld, and it may well be that for whatever reason the Earth or the inhabitants of the Otherworld may choose not to help the magician or even make themselves known to him or her, despite the fact he or she has followed all the correct procedures for making successful contact with these beings.

Usually under such circumstances the magician thinks he or she has failed or must have done something wrong, but this may not necessarily be the case. We do not always get everything we want in this world, even if we have carried out all the correct and expected procedures – so why should we automatically expect to get everything we want from the Otherworld?

Finally, if this section had been meant to describe nothing more than Bres seeking the whereabouts of his father, it would have been a simple process for Eriu just to tell him where he was instead of going through this elaborate procedure. The section also serves to remind us of the importance of listening to the feminine, intuitive side of our nature.

Section 43

The events from Section 43 onwards are happening in the Otherworld, and indicate that in this instance the inhabitants of the Otherworld have accepted the presence of Bres and Eriu. This is confirmed by the symbolic testing enacted by means of the dog race and horse race, both of which may originally have had some totemistic significance, and by the fact the Tuatha De Danann dogs and horses prove to be the better. The choice of dogs and horses may also be seen as the balance, or Polarity, between protection and aggression, in that dogs were used to protect life and property while horses were used to attack both.

We are told that the Fomoire 'sought information from them'. This indicates that the dwellers in the Otherworld are not all-knowing, but rather must rely on being told things or learning facts for themselves just as we do. They can learn as much from us as we can from them; there is always a balance in these matters.

Section 44

Section 44 deals with the testing of individuals as opposed to the testing of a whole people as seen in Section 43. The wording of this section also makes clear that there were others of the Tuatha De Danann present in the Otherworld with Bres and Eriu. This may be because Bres represents all of his people and Eriu represents the whole of Ireland. They are, in a sense, ambassadors from this world, and are consequently tested as such. This formal testing is carried out by the symbolic use of sword-play.

The sword, which represents the power and magical skills of the magician, can be seen as the 'ultimate' test of acceptability on the part of the Otherworld inhabitants. This is obviously a test which all aspiring magicians and Otherworld travellers must be willing to undergo – but there is never any guarantee of winning! In this instance Elatha recognizes the ring on Bres's finger as he is about to use his sword, and the contest is stopped before it has even begun. This can mean that Elatha accepts the obvious skills and abilities of the warrior without any need for him to compete, even though he could not identify him on a personal level.

It is important to note that Eriu is the one who answers Elatha's question concerning the identity of this warrior, and that, according to the text, 'She related to him the whole story as we have recounted it' – i.e. warts and all. This illustrates that Bres cannot continue his lying and deceitfulness in the Otherworld; his mother (or his own intuitive aspect) has to reveal the whole truth of the situation and give the real reason why they have come to the Otherworld without lies or omissions. Here is another instructive piece of information for the would-be Otherworld voyager: one's normal way of thinking and behaving is left behind on entering the Otherworld, and the purely intuitive takes over. Only the pure of heart and those with good intentions will find the Otherworld a comfortable place in which to be.

Section 45

Elatha's reaction of sorrow in Section 45 lets us know that he has indeed been told the whole truth about his son's dreadful behaviour and ineptitude. Elatha asks Bres directly for his comments on what Eriu has said, and Bres simply confirms as fact all that has been said, showing no signs of sorrow or regret – and indeed, his subsequent statements make clear his intention of carrying on with his plan of subjugating Ireland.

Section 46

Section 46 shows that the Otherworld beings have a very strong sense of justice, and will not automatically take the side of the visitor to their realms even though he or she may have successfully passed any earlier tests or questioning. It also illustrates what was said earlier about these beings not being all-knowing, as Elatha had been clearly unaware of his son's intentions and deceitful nature.

Sections 47 - 49

Sections 47 to 49 make it plain that Bres is not going to get the help he wanted nor from the source which he had expected it. On a wider, more general scale this can be seen as illustrating the fact that the schemes and plans of the Otherworld can go wrong and be upset by human interference just as easily as human plans can be disturbed by Otherworld intervention. It should be remembered at this point that the whole reason behind Elatha's coming to Eriu and lying with her was to produce a child who would be beautiful, a great king and leader of the Tuatha De Danann on all three levels.

The one unforeseeable and unpredictable factor in this whole scheme was the free will of the individual concerned, and it was this factor that neither side, or parent, could influence or affect. If Bres had turned out to be the type of individual Elatha had predicted then none of this would have happened, and our legend of the battle of Moytura would have been short indeed. This is not to be seen as a moralistic interpretation of the events related, but simply a statement of fact. We must never under any circumstances underestimate the power, for both good and bad, of individual free will.

Section 50

In Section 49 Bres puts Elatha on the spot, asking him outright for his advice on the situation. We are not given Elatha's reply, although it should be easy enough to guess. Elatha decides neither to help nor hinder Bres, passing his wayward son instead on to Balor and his Fomorian cohorts. The following section hints at the fact that Balor, Indech mac De Domnann and the Fomoire generally are not the sort of Otherworld beings that even Elatha wishes to associate with. This should be a clear warning to us that just as there are those of this world whom it is best to avoid, so too are there beings of the Otherworld who should be avoided and shunned.

We first came across Balor's name in Section 8; his reappearance here serves to keep the blood-bond between all of these various characters to the fore and thereby to link these apparently unrelated incidents. Balor is Lug's grandfather, and Lug is Bres's other half, or *Tanist*. Yet the Balor mentioned in Section 8 seemed to be an amenable enough type, so what has happened? Why is he now portrayed as a nasty sort of character?

The answer to this goes back to the original joining of the three levels, described in the opening sections of this legend. In Section 8 none of this all-important merger had taken place, therefore each race had still to encounter and join with the other two. Here in this section this triple-joining has already happened; the Fomoire are now the complementary 'dark' side to the 'light' side of the Tuatha De Danann. Polarity yet again.

This should not be confused with the modern, Christian-based concept of the opposing forces of good and evil. To the Irish Celts there were no such things as good or evil. There were events that occurred throughout life, some of which were pleasant and enjoyable and others of which were unpleasant and to be avoided if at all possible. No moral judgement was made between them, there was no concept of an ultimate good or an ultimate evil. A natural balance in all things, a constant shift in emphasis, was simply recognized and accepted. There was no need constantly to fear a total domination by evil; this would never happen. There would certainly be times when unpleasantness dominated, but it was a certainty that that time would eventually wane, to be replaced by times of pleasure, and so on in the eternal spiral which we still experience today.

An acceptance and understanding of this outlook helps greatly to explain the unpleasant and unwanted events which we all experience from time to time throughout our lives. It makes more sense to see things in this way than to accept on the one hand a God of infinite mercy yet on the other the very real problems and apparent injustices happening in the world around us.

It will be noted while studying this legend that no one ever receives praise for 'good' actions, nor is anyone ever punished for 'evil' actions. We have already read how the Dagda killed Cridenbel, but nowhere is the Dagda punished or even chastised for this action; likewise in this present passage, when Bres tells Elatha of his maltreatment of his people, Elatha's only comment is 'That is bad' – a statement of the facts as he sees them – and he simply goes on to relate how things could have been had Bres developed differently. He also neither accepts nor rejects Bres's plans to take Ireland by force, but simply passes him on to those who are more likely to be willing to assist him.

The Fomorian king Indech mac De Domnann has been mentioned in Section 25 – he is one of the three kings who imposed, through Bres, the tribute on the Tuatha De Danann, so clearly he has a personal interest in seeing Bres put back on the throne. This should be a warning that there are those of the Otherworld, just as there are of this world, who will use the magician for their own ends without the slightest consideration for the effects this will have on the individual concerned; they know only self-interest.

Section 51

Section 51 gives us the names of the places from which these mercenaries came: Lochlainn, Scythia and the Hebrides. We should not make the mistake of identifying these locations with known physical-level islands or countries, however; they are Otherworld locations, and should not be seen as anything other than this. Section 13 also mentioned the specific locations to which the Fir Bolg fled following the first battle of Moytura, all of which appeared to be close to Ireland. The locations named here, however, are much further away, and keeping in mind that they are symbolic only and not to be confused with real locations, this indicates that since the first battle of Moytura there has been a break within the ranks of the Fir Bolg and the Fomoire. This break would have occurred during the great turmoil caused by the uniting of the three levels, and is a reflection of the upset experienced by the Tuatha De Danann while coming to terms with this world. The sentence 'There was rivalry between the men . . .' tells us that they haven't ever really settled down in their new surroundings or in their new relationships with each other, for even during their united expedition to take Ireland they fight among themselves.

These Otherworld beings and locations still exist today, but it is a foolish person indeed who attempts to make any sort of conscious contact with them, for as has been made clear in the text, they are only ever interested in satisfying their own ends and have no regard or consideration for the magician stupid enough to fall under their sway. Bres was so influenced, and as we shall read, paid dearly for this further error of judgement.

Practical Work: Exercise 7

The Dagda

Go to your special place, or room, and place your Magical Weapons carefully in the centre of it. Spend a moment or two quietly closing off your day-to-day thoughts and emotions, and consciously prepare to replace them with your finer Inner processes.

When you feel ready, take your sword and mark out in a clockwise direction (either actually or symbolically depending on whether you are indoors or outdoors) the limits of your working area. Once the circle is complete you should not step outside of its limits before you formally close it at the end of the working, so make sure you have all you want and need within the circle area before you begin.

When you have completed drawing the outline of your circle, place your sword in the eastern quarter, your wand in the southern quarter, your cup in the western quarter, and your stone in the northern quarter. Return to the centre and sit, either on the ground or on a chair/stool brought previously into the circle for this purpose, and ready yourself for another Inner Journey.

As always, commence by closing down your outer awareness, perceptions and sensations. Slowly make yourself aware of your Inner senses taking over. As they open up you find yourself standing at the perimeter of a thick, deep forest, which has a look and air of great age about it. There is an abundance of bird and animal life all around you, coming and going through the forest as you stand there making yourself as real as possible in the Otherworld.

Enter the forest and start to make your way through the great mature hardwood trees. Be aware of the different types of trees there are all around you as you go deeper and deeper into the forest. How many can you name, or even recognize? See and hear the birds in and above the trees as the light from the sun high above flickers and dances and plays through the heavily-leaved branches. How many birds can you recognize? You notice little mice scurrying around the forest floor, squirrels in the branches above you, the brief flash of white as a deer lifts its fluffy tail in panic and disappears ahead of you, disturbed by the noise you are making.

As you walk through this ancient forest you realize that it is very much alive and that, at one time, you would have been quite at home here and able to blend in with all that is going on around you. Nowadays, however, you have cut yourself off so much from the Green World that you definitely feel like an intruder as you gaze in awe at the might and beauty of Nature all around you.

Presently the trees start to thin out a little, and eventually you enter into a grove of massive, ancient oak trees, in the centre of which stands a very impressive stone cairn. It sits quite naturally in this oak grove; the presence of such a huge pile of stones does not seem out of place or intrusive. As you approach this cairn you see that there is an entrance facing you. You realize that it must be hollow, or chambered, inside.

Enter into the narrow tunnel. As you do so be aware of the darkness starting to engulf you as you move slowly down the tunnel towards the centre of the cairn. At the same time be aware of your consciousness rising to a higher, more attuned state. Your eyes become accustomed to the gloom and you can make out carvings on the great stone uprights which form the walls of this tunnel: you see carvings of diamond shapes, zigzagging lines, curving lines, spirals, and many little circles and dots. Suddenly the tunnel opens out into a cross-shaped chamber with a great high ceiling which looks as though it must reach to almost the full height of the cairn. There is a recess immediately before you and to both your right and left. In each recess is a great stone basin, about two foot in diameter, filled with dark, reflective water. On the wall behind each basin is a triple spiral carving.

Go forward to the recess in front of you and gaze down into the dark surface of the water in the basin. Let your eyes softly focus on it, and clear your mind of all thoughts as much as you can. As you gaze quietly upon the water images may appear spontaneously to your Inner eye. Let them. Do not try to force any particular image, and do not try to push away any which may appear of its own accord. Simply try to remember any images which you do see, making a mental note of them. Later, when the Inner Journey is finished, note them down or draw them in your Magical Diary. They may well be of great importance to you later on.

Once you have completed this Otherworld scrying, turn around and leave the chamber through the long stone tunnel, until you find yourself standing once more outside the great stone cairn and in the centre of the oak grove. Before you but a few feet away is the figure of a large, rough-looking man dressed in a crude tunic made of animal skins. He holds in one hand a mighty wooden club, but with the other he gently strokes a little fawn, which nuzzles close to him with deep affection.

This is the Dagda, and you may ask him any questions you have relating to the powers and workings of the Green World, the world of minerals, plants and animals (which includes humanity). You may not understand all the answers he gives; this is not because he is being difficult or reluctant in opening up to you but rather indicates that your existing perceptions about the Green World are wrong. How it actually is and how you *think* it is are two very different matters.

Once you have finished your conversation with the Dagda for this session, leave the oak grove and make your way back through the thick forest until you arrive at the perimeter clearing where your Inner Journey began. Slowly and deliberately close down your Inner perceptions and replace them with your normal day-to-day senses and mode of thinking. Pick up your stone, cup, wand and then sword from the four quarters and replace them in the middle of the circle. Take your sword, go to the northern quarter, and trace out the circumference of your circle in an anti-clockwise direction. As you do so be aware of your consciousness returning fully to your normal day-to-day level, and also realize that as the circle is 'un-drawn' the temporary rift between the two worlds is once again closed.

Write up all you can remember in your Magical Diary, have a drink and a light snack, and endeavour to make any necessary changes in your attitude to the Green World which the Dagda may have indicated are advisable. Resolve to make the Green World, at least in your own immediate area, a cleaner, purer and altogether better place. This is bringing the Inner Workings into practice in this world on a very basic and necessary physical level, which is, as you know, the purpose behind all magic.

Chapter 9
Sections 52 - 71

The next block of the legend to be studied, Sections 52 to 71, is the longest so far, and is probably the most important as far as personal instruction is concerned. It deals with the reappearance of Lug, his admittance to Tara, and his taking of the throne of the High King.

Lug has only been encountered very briefly so far; the first mention of his name was in Section 4, where we were told that the spear of Lug was brought from Gorias. In Section 8 we were given Lug's lineage and the details surrounding his birth. Both of these instances were described prior to the description of the conjoining of the three levels, i.e. before the human race came to be as it is today. The third citing of Lug occurs in Section 55, when he arrives at Tara almost as a saviour figure, just when the Tuatha De Danann need someone of his abilities most.

These three instances can of course be understood as Lug travelling through the three levels until he arrives fully in the physical world, although, as will become clear, he is still very much aware of his abilities in the other two levels as well.

The passage as a whole appears in the various versions of the *Battle of Moytura* which have come down to us today, most of which are incomplete in some way, so it is clearly a very important section. It describes the personal perfection we should all be aiming for, and it shows that any one of us can become 'the glorious child' simply by reading between the lines of this and similar legends, heeding the examples, instructions and warnings given within them, and adopting the same philosophy and understanding of life as practised by the ancient Irish Celts.

The sections in question read as follows:

52. As for the Tuatha De, however, that is discussed here.
53. After Bres, Nuadu was once more in the kingship over the Tuatha De; and at that time he held a great feast for the Tuatha De in Tara. Now there was a certain warrior whose name was Samildanach on his way to Tara. At that time there were doorkeepers at Tara named Gamal mac Figail and Camall mac Riagail. While the latter was on duty, he saw the strange company coming toward him. A handsome, well-built young warrior with a king's diadem was at the front of the band.
54. They told the doorkeeper to announce their arrival in Tara. The doorkeeper said, 'Who is there?'
55. 'Lug Lonnansclech is here, the son of Cian son of Dian Cecht and of Ethne daughter of Balor. He is the foster-son of Tailtiu the daughter of Magmor, the king of Spain, and of Eochaid Garb mac Duach.'
56. The doorkeeper then asked of Samildanach, 'What art do you practice? For no one without an art enters Tara.'
57. 'Question me,' he said, 'I am a builder.'
    The doorkeeper answered, 'We do not need you. We have a builder already, Luchta mac Luachada.'
58. He said, 'Question me, doorkeeper: I am a smith.'
    The doorkeeper answered him, 'We have a smith already, Colum Cualeinech of the three new techniques.'
59. He said, 'Question me: I am a champion.'
    The doorkeeper answered, 'We do not need you. We have a champion already, Ogma mac Ethlend.'
60. He said again, 'Question me.' 'I am a harper,' he said.
    'We do not need you. We have a harper already, Abcan mac Bicelmois, whom the men of the three gods chose in the sid-mounds.'
61. He said, 'Question me: I am a warrior.'
    The doorkeeper answered, 'We do not need you. We have a warrior already, Bresal Etarlam mac Echdach Baethlaim.'

62. Then he said, 'Question me, doorkeeper. I am a poet and a historian.'

'We do not need you. We already have a poet and historian, Enmac Ethamain.'

63. He said, 'Question me. I am a sorcerer.'

'We do not need you. We have sorcerers already. Our druids and our people of power are numerous.'

64. He said, 'Question me. I am a physician.'

'We do not need you. We have Dian Cecht as a physician.'

65. 'Question me,' he said, 'I am a cupbearer.'

'We do not need you. We have cupbearers already: Delt and Drucht and Daithe, Tae and Talom and Trog, Gle and Glan and Glesse.'

66. He said, 'Question me: I am a good brazier.'

'We do not need you. We have a brazier already, Credne Cerd.'

67. He said, 'Ask the king whether he has one man who possesses all these arts: if he has I will not be able to enter Tara.'

68. Then the doorkeeper went into the royal hall and told everything to the king. 'A warrior has come before the court,' he said, 'named Samildanach; and all the arts which help your people, he practises them all, so that he is the man of each and every art.'

69. Then he said that they should bring him the fidchell-boards of Tara, and he won all the stakes, so that he made the cro of Lug. (But if fidchell was invented at the time of the Trojan War, it had not reached Ireland yet, for the battle of Mag Tuired and the destruction of Troy occurred at the same time.)

70. Then that was related to Nuadu. 'Let him come into the court,' said Nuadu, 'for a man like that has never before come into this fortress.'

71. Then the doorkeeper let him past, and he went into the fortress, and he sat in the seat of the sage, because he was a sage in every art.

The main theme of this passage is obviously the arrival of Lug at Tara and the series of tests which he has to undergo before being deemed worthy of admission. It is significant that Lug arrives immediately after Bres's

Figure 3:
The Arrival of Lug at Tara

departure to the Fomoire. He seems to be unaware of what had been taking place in Ireland prior to his arrival, however, or at any rate he never mentions it.

Putting this series of events into terms of the three levels, we could say that the spiritual aspect, Lug, has become aware of the need to make itself manifest in the physical world, Ireland (perhaps by some intuitive spiritual means he does know the trouble the Tuatha De Danann are in), and has therefore left his training in the Otherworld (symbolized by the Isle of Arran in other accounts of this same legend), and has now arrived at Tara, the spiritual centre of the physical level. The mental level is represented here by the warrior being called Samildanach, which means 'master of all crafts at once'.

Most commentators on this legend glibly assert that Lug *is* Samildanach, and carry on with this assumption without recourse to what the text actually says and without considering the all-encompassing belief in the three levels or worlds. Most researchers agree that Lug is the 'bright' or spiritual aspect of the individual and Bres the 'dark' or physical aspect, but what of the equally important mental aspect? This, in my view, is represented by Samildanach, and therefore it is an error to assume that Lug and Samildanach are one and the same, just as it is an error to assume that Lug and Bres are one and the same. It is true that they are aspects of the individual as a whole, but they nevertheless (albeit paradoxically) have an independent existence in their own right.

This may seem like unnecessary hair-splitting, but it really is an important point, and my arguments for putting it forward will become more clear as we examine this passage in more detail.

Section 52

Section 52 is simply a statement indicating that the events about to be described have shifted back to this world, and that we have temporarily left Bres, Eriu and the Fomoire in the Otherworld.

Section 53

Section 53 contains a great deal of information, much of which sets the scene for later important events. The first point to note is that Nuadu is back on the throne. He is holding a great feast at Tara for the Tuatha De Danann. As Nuadu was always intended to be king this implies that balance has been restored in the physical world, something also indicated later, in Section 59, when we see Ogma has been restored to his rightful position as champion of his people. The reversal of roles we have encountered up until now has ended. This does, however, also indicate that the Tuatha De Danann are unaware of Bres's actions in the Otherworld and the impending invasion by the Fomorian host, who are already on their way to taking Ireland by force.

This points out one of the great dangers for those living too much in the physical world - the inability, at times, to see past the immediate events occurring at this level, and the consequent ignorance of events happening concurrently on the other two levels. The Tuatha De Danann, in this instance, must have earlier deposed Bres in favour of Nuadu, yet they seem to have ignored the obvious possibility of Bres seeking revenge or compensation for his removal from the position he so dearly coveted. Lug, the higher, more intuitive aspect of the Tuatha De Danann, does fortunately seem to have become aware of this danger, and has left his Otherworld abode to come to the assistance of his people.

In terms of the three levels again, this means that the purely spiritual aspect of a people, its divine aspect in this context, has voluntarily given itself a physical incarnation, with all its inherent dangers and limitations, in order to save the people from destroying themselves. This basic theme is the central belief behind most of the world religions today, and is clearly one that the unconscious part of the human psyche, the mental level if you like, in the case of all races and peoples, recognizes and responds to. The reverse of course must also be true - that a physical being can manifest or 'incarnate' into the spiritual realms; this, once more, is a basic belief and forms part of many of this world's religions and creeds.

Returning to our examination of Section 53, however, we should pay particular attention to the second sentence, as it is here we get our first indication that Lug and Samildanach are not one and the same person. The sentence reads, 'Now there was a certain warrior whose name was Samildanach on his way to Tara.' It does not therefore specifically name or mention Lug. If the warrior were intended to be understood as Lug this would be out of keeping with the rest of the narrative. Throughout this legend people of importance are always introduced by being named specifically and either their function or their lineage given. Lug, in this case, has already been named as one of the keepers of the Treasures of the Tuatha De Danann, and was described in Section 8 as 'the glorious child'. To refer to him now in the glib terms of 'a certain warrior' just when he is about to play his most important part seems completely inconsistent with the rest of the text.

It is also important to understand that Samildanach is not a personal name but rather a title that means something like 'master of all crafts at one time'. It was the custom in those days for a king or visitor of importance to send ahead heralds announcing his imminent arrival in order that the host could make suitable arrangements for hospitality according to the guest's status. The status was indicated by the heralds being given some token of their master's position, and this is confirmed in the text where we are told that this warrior had with him a king's diadem.

It was the custom at Tara not to admit anyone into the hall once feasting had commenced; doorkeepers were put in position to ensure this rule was not broken. Doorkeepers held a very high position in ancient Celtic society, and were definitely not regarded as menial workers such as we would most likely consider them today. The name Camall mac Riagail means 'Sober, son of Rule'; Gamal mac Figail means 'Simpleton, son of Vigilance'. We should not apply the modern meaning of the word simpleton to this important character, for what is actually implied here is one who is inspired by divine madness. Such people are even today regarded as being spiritually enlightened according to some Eastern religions, and even in the West it is generally agreed that there can exist a thin line between genius and madness. Gamal's father was in fact a druid called Figol mac Mamois, a name that means 'Vigil, son of Subservience'. In short, from their very names we can see that these doorkeepers were suitably skilled for their important function and were men of some standing.

This should be an indication to Otherworld voyagers that anyone encountered who takes on the role of doorkeeper or questioner is in fact extremely important and must be treated as such. This can also apply to some present-day magical and occult groups, whose apparent head or leader 'interviews' hopeful applicants when in fact the real interview has already been carried out by the person who opened the door or served the coffee prior to the 'main' interview. The purpose behind this is not deliberate deceit or trickery but the simple psychological fact that we tend to be more at ease, and therefore more revealing about ourselves, with people we consider our equals or even of little importance than with someone we consider our superior or our interrogator.

Section 54

Sections 54 to 66 are the first of a series of three symbolic and ritualistic questionings that occur in this legend, the other two coming later in the text as the plans for the second battle of Moytura are being drawn up. This first set of questions is aimed at testing the entrant to Tara on a physical level; the other two enact a similar process but on the mental and spiritual levels respectively. This again contains information for the Otherworld voyager – you must be prepared for such a journey on all three levels, and you must be prepared to be tested on each of those levels. The questions and answers given in the text are very rigid and formal; this indicates the ritualistic nature of the questioning.

Section 54 itself is self-explanatory, but it should be noted that there is obviously more than one person who has arrived in Tara. Section 53 describes 'the strange company' and 'the band', and here we have, 'They told the doorkeeper to announce their arrival in Tara.' Clearly Lug and Samildanach are not alone.

Section 55

Section 55 gives another indication that Lug and Samildanach are not meant to be one and the same person. After announcing Lug's full name and lineage in the first sentence, the speaker, Samildanach, then starts the second sentence with, 'He is the foster-son of', and not '*I am the foster-son*', as we would expect if the speaker was referring to himself.

We already know of Lug's blood relatives, but it is interesting to note the identity of his foster-parents. Fosterage in Celtic society was a common and very important practice, and the loyalty and devotion shown foster-parents was as strong if not stronger than that shown natural parents. Lug's foster-mother (note the emphasis here on matrilinear descent) was Tailtiu, the daughter of Magmor, king of Spain; Lug's foster-father was Eochaid Garb mac Duach. Tailtiu was of the Fir Bolg, Eochaid Garb mac Duach of the Tuatha De Danann, and Lug's natural mother, Ethne, of the Fomoire. Thus all three races were involved in one way or another in the raising of Lug.

From other sources we also know that Eochaid was Tailtiu's second husband, her first being another Eochaid, Eochaid mac Eirc, who was the Fir Bolg king defeated during the first battle of Moytura (see Section 10, page 65). Lug can therefore be seen to be a perfected being on all levels, incorporating a significant part of each of the three races in his make-up as well as the important duality, or Polarity aspect, as manifest by his Tanist, Bres.

Tailtiu's father is called 'king of Spain'; this is a reference to the Otherworld and not the present country which we call Spain. We know from other legends that Lug spent his childhood in Arran, which was also considered to be of the Otherworld. Taking all of these factors into account we can see that this stranger who arrives at Tara with his 'strange company' is a very important visitor indeed. His champion, or herald, who announces his arrival to the doorkeepers, must likewise be a very special person, and

is, as we have indicated, the third aspect of the composite
triple being of Lug/Bres/Samildanach.

Section 56

Section 56 confirms that it is Samildanach speaking to the
doorkeepers and not Lug himself. The doorkeeper at this
stage obviously does not know who this stranger is,
although the herald has announced Lug's (his master's)
name. If the doorkeeper knew the herald was
Samildanach, 'master of all arts at once', he would not have
proceeded to ask him which art he practised; his very
name would have answered that question immediately.
This of course reinforces what was said earlier about
Otherworld beings not being all-knowing – they need
information from us just as we often need information
from them.

Section 57

Section 57 begins the very formal, ritualistic series of
questions and answers, the purpose of which is to decide
whether this herald, and therefore his master's company,
are worthy of entering Tara, the spiritual centre of all
Ireland. Note that Samildanach always starts by saying,
'Question me', yet the doorkeeper never does. He simply
responds in a negative way to Samildanach's statements.
   The first art Samildanach declares himself to be master
of is that of building. The word that translates into English
as 'builder' actually has a fuller meaning in Old Irish,
implying more of a craftsman in all materials. This is
expressed, in a fashion, by the builder whom the
doorkeeper names, Luchta mac Luachada. We will find in
Section 103, making shields and spearshafts, and then
again in Section 122 where he is described as Luchta the
Carpenter. He is obviously not just proficient with
building materials alone.

Section 58

In Section 58 Samildanach declares himself to be a smith,
but in reply the doorkeeper does not start with his usual,

'We do not need you', but rather simply names the smith they already have, Colum Cualeinech 'of the three new techniques'. We are not told what these new techniques are, but the fact that Colum, a relatively obscure member of the Tuatha De Danann is named as their main smith, as opposed to the better known Goibniu and Credne Cerd, may indicate that these techniques were ones found to be better suited to the physical world, in which the Tuatha De Danann now had their being, than those of Goibniu or Credne Cerd, which were older and maybe only suited to the other two levels. Whatever the intended meaning behind all this, the doorkeeper still does not admit Samildanach to Tara.

Section 59

Section 59 returns to the straightforward naming of a craft and the 'We do not need you' reply. The craft named this time is that of champion which, as will be seen later, was looked upon as being a separate art from that of warrior.

This list of arts and crafts tells us a good deal about the structure of contemporary Celtic society, as well as which skills and abilities were considered useful and important. The existing champion of the Tuatha De Danann, according to the doorkeeper, was Ogma mac Ethlend, whom we met in a previous passage (see Chapter 7). In that earlier passage he was called Ogma the son of Etain, and was performing the menial task of gathering firewood, but clearly he has now been restored to his rightful position, probably because Nuadu is back on the throne and things have returned to normal.

Section 60

Section 60 raises a few issues, including (again) the apparent anachronism of the 'sid-mounds', which we discussed briefly in our analysis of Section 41. The 'men of the three gods' is a new concept - a full discussion of it, however, is beyond the scope of this book. This title crops us in several other legends, although we are never told who the three gods in question actually are. It is known that the Celts were reluctant to name their deities specifically, especially to non-Celts, and a common oath was 'I swear by the gods my people swear by'; this may have some bearing on this peculiar title. The important point, though, is that Samildanach's harp-playing abilities are not needed, as Abcan mac Bicelmois does the job already. As he is described as having been chosen from the sid-mounds we are obviously meant to understand he was of the Otherworld; the musical abilities of the Otherworld harpers were legendary. Music, and therefore musicians, were extremely important to the Celts, and it was also held to be a magical ability. This will be demonstrated later.

Section 61

Section 61 tells us that there was a difference between a champion, as named in Section 59, and a warrior. It is curious to note that the doorkeeper does not tell Samildanach they do not need him as they already have many warriors, as would be expected among a warrior-people, but instead only identifies and names one specific warrior, Bresal Etarlam mac Echdach Baethlaim. Unfortunately we know nothing about this character at all. It is reasonable to assume that he must have had some significance at one time if he is specifically mentioned at this important point in the legend, but sadly we no longer know what that significance was.

Section 62

Section 62 contains the usual rebuff, but at least lets us know that among the Celts poetry went hand in hand with the telling and recording of history. The field of history probably took the form of studying genealogical lists and accounts of individual bravery and valour on the battlefield, both of which were of great importance to the Celts. It is also curious to note that the poet named, En mac Ethamain, is not the same poet of the Tuatha De Danann we encountered earlier, namely Coirpre son of Etain. This once again may be due to the change of king from Bres to Nuadu, which thereby restored the previously lost order of society.

Section 63

Section 63 is the only section in this series of questions and answers where although Samildanach is rebuffed as usual we are not given any specific names. In fact what we are told is that they do not need a sorcerer, as they already have 'numerous' people skilled in the magical arts. This is of course the way things were when this legend started back in Section 1, when all of the Tuatha De Danann were in the northern islands of the world learning magical arts and skills. This illustrates the importance these beings represent to those of us who wish to become masters of the magical arts, and is the reason why journeys to the Otherworld are necessary if any sort of progress is to be made within the Irish Celtic tradition.

Section 64

Section 64 tells us that Dian Cecht is still the physician of the Tuatha De Danann; therefore Samildanach's medical skills are not required. This section also adds weight to my argument that Lug and Samildanach are not one and the same, because as we already know Dian Cecht is Lug's grandfather, and if Lug had been standing at the door to Tara he would hardly have needed to be reminded of the fact that his own grandfather was a physician, let alone try to gain entrance by naming an art that he knew the Tuatha De Danann would not need from him.

Section 65

Section 65 may seem a bit odd to us. After naming so many highly valuable and complicated skills, Samildanach tries to gain admittance on the fact he is a cupbearer. The significance of this is lost on us today, unless we remember that apparently menial positions, such as doorkeeper and cupbearer, were in fact of a very high magical order and were regarded with a great deal of respect. The symbolism behind the cup in all magical systems and traditions is enormous, and the bearer of this magical device held a tremendous responsibility.

Instead of naming one specific cupbearer, the doorkeeper actually names nine, three sets of three, in a strange, rhyming reply which hints at the importance and ritualistic nature of these cupbearers. Some of their names are obscure, but we know 'Drucht' means 'dew'; 'Daithe' means 'swiftness, light'; 'Tae' means 'birth'; 'Talom' means 'earth, speedy'; 'Trog' means 'offspring'; 'Gle' means 'clear, evident'; 'Glan' means 'clean, pure' and 'Glesse' means 'brightness'. Their names therefore express magical properties and attributes, and the fact that they are recited as three sets of three also emphasizes their magical significance and importance. I would suggest that encountering one or all of these cupbearers during an Otherworld journey could be very fruitful to the trainee magician.

Section 66

Section 66 returns to the straightforward naming of a skill and the reply of 'We do not need you. We have a brazier already', in this case Credne Cerd. We have already encountered Credne Cerd at the start of this legend, and need not say anything further about him here.

Section 67

Section 67 sees the end of this very formal series of questions and answers, yet despite the fact Samildanach has not been able to come up with one skill which the Tuatha De Danann actually need he seems very confident, and has clearly passed this first of a series of measures of his worthiness. He confidently tells his questioner, the doorkeeper, to ask the king if there is already one man among the Tuatha De Danann who possesses all of the aforementioned arts at once. The fact that the doorkeeper himself cannot answer this question but must go to the king indicates that the doorkeeper's testing function has now ceased, and that Samildanach must now move on to the next level of testing.

Samildanach realizes that should there already be such a person within Tara he will be unable to enter, despite his great skills and Otherworld status. This shows that he must abide by the laws and conventions of the physical level upon which he is now operating. The reverse is also the case and must be borne in mind by those of this world who learn the skill of operating consciously in the Otherworld. There are many different laws and rules governing the Otherworld, and you must obey and comply with them if you are to be accepted there and be successful in your ventures. Some of these Otherworld rules and conditions have already been given in this text, and more are still to be revealed. It is important to note them and abide by them.

Section 68

Section 68 tells us that the doorkeeper goes to the king, relates what has happened so far - i.e. that the stranger has passed the first test - and then leaves it for the king to decide what is to be done next. It should be noted that the doorkeeper tells the king, 'all the arts which help your people, he practises them all'. In other words Samildanach does not bring anything new to Tara; he does not claim to be able to do something nobody else can do, nor does he claim to be better at any of the existing arts than the king's own people. His own claim to the right of admission is that he, and he alone, can practise all arts at the same time.

This can be read as saying that there are no new skills to be brought to Tara and also that all skills exist, in some form or another, on all three levels. For Samildanach, and his other aspects of Lug and Bres, are conscious operators on all three levels at once. This serves to emphasize what was said at the start of this examination of *The Battle of Moytura*, that although there are three levels no single one should be considered as being better than any other, they are all equal in importance and stature.

The doorkeeper announces the arrival of Samildanach

and not his master Lug to the king, and this lets us know
that further testing is still to be carried out before the
whole party can be deemed worthy of entering Tara.

Section 69

Section 69 commences this next round of testing.
Whereas the previous test had been on the physical level
(questions about personal abilities and skills), this next
testing is, as we would expect, on the mental level, and
takes the form of a popular board-game of the day called
'fidchell'. Fidchell literally means 'wood knowledge'; we
know nothing of its structure or rules other than it seemed
to have been similar in nature to chess. The name itself
may hint at a druidical origin, for it is known that the
druids used trees in many symbolic and magical ways.
This test may in fact have been used to ascertain just how
much of this important druidical tree-lore Samildanach
possessed.

Samildanach passes this test as well, and does so by
virtue of the fact that 'he made the cro of Lug', which
presumably was a move or series of moves credited as
having first been used or invented by Lug. The word 'cro'
means an enclosure or pen, and this would be a good
description for a move, even in modern chess, which
resulted in the king or most valuable piece being enclosed
or penned-in so that it could not escape. The same word
was used to describe the circular wall of spears put up by
warriors during battle as an impenetrable barrier: this too
has a connection with Lug if we remember that the
magical weapon of Lug is the spear which was brought
from Gorias.

The last part of this section refers to the Trojan War, and
is therefore clearly another addition made by the
Christian scribes who set the legend down in writing. As
is usually the case with such additions, however, it does
not actually change the sense or meaning of what we have
just been told, and in fact its only purpose was to put some
sort of known date on the events being described. Such
dating was always made by reference to a known Biblical
or classical historical event.

Section 70

Section 70 tells us that the news of Samildanach's second success in this round of testing was brought to Nuadu, which indicates that the game of fidchell was not played against Nuadu himself, as is usually assumed, but against some other unnamed adversary. This once more hints at the fact that Samildanach is not meant to be Lug, for if Lug himself had played the game, then by the laws of courtesy and status he would have had to have been matched by his equal, who in this instance would have been Nuadu himself.

On hearing this news Nuadu says, 'Let him come into the court', i.e. not just into Tara but into the inner part of Tara, the spiritual centre of the Spiritual Centre, where the final testing, to take place on the spiritual level, will occur. The first, the physical test took place outside Tara; the second, the mental test took place within the walls of Tara but not within its inner sanctum, and this final, spiritual test will take place within the very heart of Tara, the High King's Court. This then is yet another symbolic representation of progress through the three levels; a theme which will recur throughout this legend and which serves to stress the extreme importance of the concept of advancement. It is also intended to portray the several ways in which improvement may be accomplished by the individual.

Section 71

Section 71 is where we are told that the company were finally let into Tara. Samildanach, now that his testing is over, takes his rightful place in the seat of the sage. This of course means that the final test must be taken by Lug himself, he cannot delegate it to his champion Samildanach as has been the case up until now. This is still so today, where we can use or ask others to do almost anything on a physical or mental level on our behalf, but when it comes to matters relating to the spiritual level we are on our own; nobody can do those for us.

This is one of the basic tenets of the Irish system, and

one which places an enormous responsibility on the individual. If the individual cannot face up to this responsibility, or is weak and fails the tests of the other two levels, then he or she will not make any spiritual progress.

In a sense this is not as final as it seems. On his or her death the person who has failed for whatever reason to achieve spiritual progress during incarnation will still travel on to the Otherworld (remember, there is no concept of Divine Reward or Punishment in this system). Once in the Otherworld a person can then decide whether to remain there in that state or to return to this world in another incarnation and have another go at spiritual advancement.

Practical Work: Exercise 8

Ogma

Prepare your working area and open your circle as in the last exercise, sit in the centre and visualize the following Inner Journey.

When your Inner senses take over you find yourself standing in bright sunlight in the middle of what at first seems to be a camp of rough tents and shelters about to prepare for war. There are many armed men and women moving around the encampment, which is quite large, and you can hear from somewhere not too far off the sound of weapons clashing and people grunting and straining under force of arms. After a moment you realize that there is no air of panic or hurry in the encampment as there would be if the people were really at war, and you realize that this is actually a military training area.

You stroll among the various tents and shelters and see not only warriors preparing weapons and doing physical exercises but also craftspeople making and repairing various weapons, swords, shields, axes and so on. A couple of tents have been set aside to treat those accidentally injured during their training, these are nearest to the training area itself. It is from the training area itself that the various noises you heard earlier emanate, and on a patch of hard bare earth several men and women are

challenging each other with swords and also with hand-to-
hand combat. There is quite a confusion of men and
women running, stumbling and being pushed in all
directions, and you wonder at the fact that no one has got
seriously injured.

As you gaze upon this strange scene you realize that
there is one figure who is not fighting but who carefully
makes his way through the battling bodies, as if watching
them all and studying who is doing what. Presently he
holds aloft a great shield and strikes it hard several times
with a short stabbing sword. It makes a dreadful din and
immediately everybody stops fighting, some falling
exhausted to their knees, and he makes comments to
various individuals and suggests improvements each can
make in his or her fighting technique. Once all necessary
instructions have been given the warriors turn and leave
the training area and go to their tents for a well earned rest.

The instructor lays his sword and shield on the earth
and walks over to you, his face expressionless and hard.
This is Ogma, the Champion of the Tuatha De Danann,
and it is to him you must turn if you wish to learn matters
pertaining to your own development and abilities and how
best to utilize that which you are naturally good at and
how best to improve that which you are naturally poor at.
Although you have just witnessed Ogma giving advice on
purely physical development you should understand that
his counsel is available to you on any matter relating to
self-improvement and advancement, not just on a physical
level. This is your first opportunity to discuss such
matters with him.

As always in these situations, you must realize that
Ogma is very real and that he will have words to give you.
The secret is to pacify your own thoughts and
anticipations sufficiently for Ogma to make himself heard
within your own mind. Do not try to anticipate what he -
or any other Otherworld guide or contact - may say. You
do not try to put words into the mouths of friends and
acquaintances but rather ask your questions, make your
comments, and await their own words of reply. So too on
the Inner levels.

Once you have received his answers to your questions
you should thank Ogma for his help and advice and make

your way back to this world. Never stay in the Otherworld longer than you really need to. It is not advisable to make these Inner Journeys just for the 'fun' of it. Always have a specific purpose for going there and always keep that purpose in mind once you are there.

To close this session for the time being make your way back through the encampment to the spot where your Inner Journey commenced. Return your consciousness in the usual way to its full day-to-day state, close your circle in the usual manner and finish off by writing up your experience in your Magical Diary and closing down your Inner senses completely with the aid of a little food and drink.

Chapter 10
Sections 72 - 82

The sections which follow, 72 to 82, continue the testing of Lug and his company and give us a description of the preparations the Tuatha De Danann are making for battle with the Fomoire. As is always the case in interpreting the legend it can be read on three levels - the obvious or surface level, which is simply an account of the preparations for battle; on a slightly deeper level, as an allegory of human behaviour and relationships; and on a deeper level still, as a description of the trials and tests facing the individual during his or her journey through life before he or she can be called Samildanach. The sections read as follows:

72. Then Ogma threw the flagstone, which required fourscore yoke of oxen to move it, through the side of the hall so that it lay outside against Tara. That was to challenge Lug, who tossed the stone back so that it lay in the centre of the royal hall; and he threw the piece which it had carried away back into the side of the royal hall so that it was whole again.

73. 'Let a harp be played for us,' said the hosts. Then the warrior played sleep music for the hosts and for the king on the first night, putting them to sleep from that hour to the same time the next day. He played sorrowful music so that they were crying and lamenting. He played joyful music so that they were merry and rejoicing.

74. Then Nuadu, when he had seen the warrior's many

powers, considered whether he could release them
from the bondage they suffered at the hands of the
Fomoire. So they held a council concerning the
warrior, and the decision which Nuadu reached was to
exchange seats with the warrior. So Samildanach went
to the king's seat, and the king arose before him until
thirteen days had passed.

75. The next day he and the two brothers, Dagda and
Ogma, conversed together on Grellach Dollaid; and his
two kinsmen Goibniu and Dian Cecht were
summoned to them.

76. They spent a full year in that secret conference, so that
Grellach Dollaid is called the Amrun of the Men of the
Goddess.

77. Then the druids of Ireland were summoned to them,
together with their physicians and their charioteers
and their smiths and their wealthy landowners and
their lawyers. They conversed together secretly.

78. Then he asked the sorcerer, whose name was Mathgen,
what power he wielded. He answered that he would
shake the mountains of Ireland beneath the Fomoire
so that their summits would fall to the ground. And
it would seem to them that the twelve chief
mountains of the land of Ireland would be fighting on
behalf of the Tuatha De Danann; Slieve League, and
Denda Ulad, and the Mourne Mountains, and Bri Erigi
and Slieve Bloom and Slieve Snaght, Slemish and
Blaisliab and Nephin Mountain and Sliab Maccu
Belgodon and the Curlieu hills and Croagh Patrick.

79. Then he asked the cupbearer what power he wielded.
He answered that he would bring the twelve chief
lochs of Ireland into the presence of the Fomoire and
they would not find water in them, however thirsty
they were. These are the lochs: Lough Derg, Lough
Luimnig, Lough Corrib, Lough Ree, Lough Mask,
Strangford Lough, Belfast Lough, Lough Neagh, Lough
Foyle, Lough Gara, Loughrea, Marloch. They would
proceed to the twelve chief rivers of Ireland – the Bush,
the Boyne, the Bann, the Blackwater, the Lee, the
Shannon, the Moy, the Sligo, the Erne, the Finn, the
Liffey, the Suir – and they would all be hidden from the
Fomoire so they would not find a drop in them. But

drink will be provided for the men of Ireland even if they remain in battle for seven years.

80. Then Figol mac Mamois, their druid, said, 'Three showers of fire will be rained upon the faces of the Fomorian host, and I will take out of them two-thirds of their courage and their skill at arms and their strength, and I will bind their urine in their own bodies and in the bodies of their horses. Every breath that the men of Ireland will exhale will increase their courage and skill at arms and strength. Even if they remain in battle for seven years, they will not be weary at all.'

81. The Dagda said, 'The power which you boast, I will wield it all myself.'

'You are the Dagda ('the Good God')!' said everyone; and Dagda stuck to him from that time on.

82. Then they disbanded the council to meet that day three years later.

Section 72

This block of the text begins with the spiritual testing of Lug, which takes the form of a challenge made by Ogma, the throwing of the flagstone. In the first two tests a wrong answer during the questioning or a wrong move during the fidchell game would have resulted in failure, but such a failure would only have been on a personal level, and the contender could go away, study more and eventually come back and try again. In this final test, however, there is only one chance, and failure at this level is a much more serious matter.

The mighty flagstone at the centre of Tara which took fourscore yoke of oxen to move is in fact the Lia Fail, first introduced in Section 3. This description of it is not intended to convey a sense of great physical weight but more great spiritual weight or importance. The fact that Ogma throws it with apparent ease shows that its physical weight should not necessarily be a hindrance in lifting it, although its spiritual weight could prevent certain individuals from doing so. In other words, only those spiritually pure and advanced are capable of lifting it.

This is exactly the same motif as that found in the Arthurian legend, where only the true king, and hence spiritually pure person, could remove the sword from the stone.

Ogma can handle the stone easily because he is a first-generation member of the Tuatha De Danann and has come to this world directly from the Otherworld; he is therefore adept at working with the powers of the spiritual level. Lug, on the other hand, is second-generation Tuatha De Danann, and although he has come from the Otherworld, his spiritual abilities have still to be proven and tested. The second sentence of Section 72 states specifically that the challenge is directed at Lug, and not at 'the warrior' or 'Samildanach' as has been the case until now. In fact this is the first section in which Lug actually takes part, and as we have already been told that Samildanach is having a well-earned rest in the seat of the sage, it is plain that Lug and Samildanach are definitely not one and the same being. They are, however, separate aspects of the same whole, as has been noted.

Lug passes this test with flying colours, even managing to repair the damage done to the royal hall by Ogma, who threw the stone through its wall. This tells us not only that the spiritual powers are capable of causing damage on the physical level but that, consequently, those capable of handling the spiritual powers can use them to effect repairs on the physical level as well.

This also serves as a warning that anyone who goes as far as facing up to their own spiritual testing must be prepared for challenges not only on the spiritual but on the physical level as well. As we can infer from the text, these physical tests may well take the form of severe damage or upset to our day-to-day lives. This must be fully realized and understood by those contemplating taking up this system of magic and spiritual development. The tests on the way are very real indeed and, by their very nature, will push you until you think you have had more than enough and are ready for breaking. It is by no means an easy course to follow, and its challenges can be very hard and painful indeed. Think carefully about your own intentions and abilities before going to the Hall of Tara and facing this final, and most severe, test.

Section 73

Section 73 describes the celebrations and resting after Lug's success and the acceptance of the company into Tara. The text reverts back to using the title 'the warrior'; this refers to Samildanach again, and not Lug. Under the rules of hospitality and diplomacy Nuadu, a king, would not have asked Lug, a fellow king, to provide the entertainment in his own hall. Samildanach has already professed his prowess on the harp (Section 60), and it is fair to conclude, as has been argued all along, that Lug and Samildanach are not one and the same person.

The three types of music played – sleeping, sorrowful and joyful – crop up many times in the Irish legends, and serve to illustrate the universally applicable principle of the three levels, even in music, and also to hint at music's magical properties, as mentioned earlier.

Section 74

Section 74 brings our attention back to the impending battle with the Fomoire. We should note that the text tells us 'they held a council concerning the warrior', which reminds us that the king did not have ultimate say in all matters but had to refer back to his people, or their representatives, and obtain their agreement and permission to go ahead with any plans which might affect them all.

The last sentence of this section has caused a lot of comment and debate among scholars, centred around exactly what it implies and why a period of thirteen days is involved. If the legend is read on a superficial level only, then no doubt this exchange of positions between Nuadu and Samildanach will seem confusing and pointless. For those of us who can read deeper than just the surface meaning, however, it makes a lot of sense and also indicates that a very powerful, and as it turns out prolonged, magical ritual is about to begin.

The replacing of the king by a substitute was not an uncommon act in Celtic society, and was carried out on several occasions. Often it was done by way of a symbolic self-sacrifice, although in later years this sometimes turned into an actual sacrifice. More usually it was done for magical reasons, as is the case here. The period of thirteen days is also symbolic, as it can be seen to represent a whole year if each day is understood to represent a Lunar month. Later in this passage the number twelve crops up a few times; this can also be seen as a year, this time with each day representing a Solar month. Lunar months were used to mark time for magical purposes, for those events that took place mainly on an Inner level, while Solar months were used to mark time for the events of this world. By identifying Lunar months at this point we are given an indication that the events to follow are of an Inner, magical nature.

There is, however, a more subtle aspect to the mention of a period of thirteen days, an aspect lost to most of us nowadays but which would have been of great significance to the ancient Celtic listener to this tale. The Celts of Ireland, when this legend was formulated, counted time in 'weeks' consisting of nine nights. The Celts considered a period of twenty-four hours to commence with dusk on one day and end with dusk on the other, i.e. they counted in nights and not days as we do now. This nine-night period was then split into segments consisting of five nights and four days respectively and known as a 'noinden'. The last night of one noinden was therefore the first night of the succeeding noinden; this displayed both the important principle of Polarity, there being two noinden in each period, and also of 'in-between-ness', there being one night which was in-between both noindens. The same principle applied on a grander scale with the passage of time throughout the year, where the actual days on which the festivals of Beltaine and Samhain began were considered outside time as they were in-between winter and summer, summer and winter respectively.

If you consider a period of three noinden, one for each of the three levels (and in essence the whole of creation), it will be seen that such a period of time will consist of thirteen nights, and consequently thirteen days. This period was therefore not only symbolic of the passing of the year but also of the three levels and, by implication, of everything that exists on all three levels.

The exchanging of the king with the 'master of all arts at once' for a period which symbolized the whole of time and everything in creation indicates that a most powerful ritual is underway. The purpose behind this ritual was to defend Ireland, and therefore the entire physical world, from the invading Fomorian menace - a purpose indeed of the utmost importance.

This impending second battle of Moytura is the Polar or balancing aspect of the first battle. In that first battle the Tuatha De Danann came to Ireland and took it by force from the native population; now the Fomoire are arriving in great numbers with exactly the same intention. This reflects the inescapable principle that everything is in a permanent state of flux and shift of emphasis from one pole to the other. It is vital to recognize this principle and understand it if you are ever to make any headway in your magical studies or, on a more mundane level, to make any sense of this apparently nonsensical world in which we live.

Yet another motif involving threes is taking place at this stage. The threes involved are the three takings of seats. The first is in Section 71 when Samildanach takes the seat of the sage, the second is in Section 74 when Samildanach takes the seat, or throne, of Nuadu, and the third occurs after the battle, when Lug takes the throne of the Tuatha De Danann on the death of Nuadu (Section 133). As is always the case this can be read on a more personal basis, and indicates a movement or progression through the three levels. Taking the seat, or throne, means being fully in charge of that level, just as the king or throned-one is in charge of his or her realm or world.

Section 75

Section 75 sees the ritual proper commencing, with the necessary preliminary discussions and clarifications taking place. The opening sections of this legend were concerned with the three levels of creation - a triplicity - calling into being the two aspects - or duality - of physical manifestation; all this was immediately followed by a great battle. Here exactly the same scenario is described, but on a lesser scale – a triplicity (Lug, the Dagda and Ogma) calls forth a duality (Goibniu and Dian Cecht), and soon a great battle will follow. The ritual which is about to follow must be of major significance, as it looks as though its purpose is to mirror the very act of creation itself.

Goibniu is a new character, and he is Dian Cecht's brother. All of the participants in this great ritual are closely related to one another, as has been the case all along so far. His craft is that of the smith, and later in the battle he plays a crucial role, using his skills to repair the warriors' broken weapons.

Section 76

Section 76 confirms that all this is of a ritualistic nature by introducing the word 'Amrun'. This word is actually composed of two words, 'am' which means 'time or occasion' and 'run' which means 'magical chants'. An Amrun, then, is a time of magical chanting – or, in more modern parlance, a ritual. The reference to the conference lasting one year is an indication that the events are occurring in the Otherworld where, as we have noted, time passes at a very different rate than it does in our world.

Section 77

Section 77 tells us that the ritual is now well underway. The conference, which involved the five participants in Section 75, must have centred around the nature of the ritual to follow. Now that this has been decided all of the rest of the Tuatha De Danann, symbolized by the unnamed individuals of differing status and occupations, have been called forth to participate. The final sentence of this section, 'They conversed together secretly', indicates yet again the magical nature of this gathering, for two reasons. First, this meeting cannot be 'secret' in the usual sense of the word when it involves all of the Tuatha De Danann, and second, the four great tenets of any worthwhile magician are To Know, To Will, To Dare and

To Keep Silent (or secret, as it were).

This structure, of the five very important Tuatha De Danann starting off the ritual and then involving all of their people later, is one that occurs to this day within most serious magical groups and orders. Such groups are usually made up of a small band of Adepts, called the Inner Temple, who decide on the magical Work needing to be done and exactly how to go about it, and of the main body of the group, called the Outer Temple, who are used to provide the numbers and energy necessary for successful group magical Working. In some groups and orders there is also a high degree of secrecy, even to the extent that some of the Outer Temple grades are unaware of the very existence of the Inner Temple.

Section 78

Section 78 begins the second ritualistic set of questions and answers, the first having been the challenges made to Samildanach on his arrival at Tara. This time the questioner would appear to be Lug, who is now in charge of the ritual in hand.

The sorcerer's name, Mathgen, is composed of two words meaning 'one who bears or gives birth' and 'soothsayer or diviner', which could be put into English as 'one who utters prophecies'. This is exactly what he proceeds to do. Presumably Mathgen must be a sorcerer of some ability, although it is interesting to note that the things he claims he will do to aid the battle all involve the use and co-operation of the natural Earth forces and energies. He does not intend to use some ethereal 'high' magic involving the forces and energies of the other levels, but prefers instead to use those which are immediately surrounding him and available to him.

It may well be he does this because of the close affinity between the Tuatha De Danann and the physical earth of Ireland itself (which is, after all, what is at stake in the forthcoming battle). This link is emphasized in this section, where it is said, 'the twelve chief mountains of the land of Ireland would be fighting on behalf of the Tuatha De Danann'. This should serve as a reminder to the newcomer to the magical arts that it is not always necessary, nor desirable, to go for the 'highest' and most spectacular form of magic available. Use the one which is best suited to the matter in hand.

The symbolism behind these twelve mountains has been lost to us today, and the naming of the mountain Croagh Patrick, obviously a later Christian embellishment or amendment, reflects the fact that even at the time this legend was set down in writing the full significance of the twelve mountains had already been forgotten; clearly it is of no real consequence anyway. The main point behind this section remains clear: the Tuatha De Danann are going to use the natural Earth energies to oppose the Otherworld warriors of the Fomoire, and that is all that matters. There are many sections and passages in this legend which are now obscure or incomprehensible to us, but this is as it should be. Whatever relevance the mountains named had to the Celt of a thousand years ago has long since died, and there is no point in spending time and energy trying to understand or decipher symbolism which is of no use to us today. Magic like everything else on this planet is organic in nature, and goes through the same basic process of evolution and change as everything else. It is going against the very laws of Nature to try to bring back something that Nature has decided is obsolete and must be broken down so that its component parts can be re-used for something new and useful.

Section 79

Section 79 continues the questioning of specific members of the Tuatha De Danann. This time it is the cupbearer who declares what his part in the battle will be. We noted earlier that the seemingly humble position of cupbearer is in fact a very important office; this is more than confirmed here by the revelation that the cupbearer is in charge of the very waters, rivers and lochs of Ireland. The magical use of thirst against an enemy is a common theme in Irish legends, as is its opposite, the giving of water by one individual to another. Again this displays the very close links between the magical powers of the Tuatha De

Danann and the natural powers and resources of this Earth. As with the mountains, the significance of the rivers and lochs that are named has been lost to us. The mention of a period of seven years, as noted earlier, is purely symbolic and not intended to be understood literally.

Section 80

Section 80 is the last set of questions and answers in this passage. They are directed at the druid Figol mac Mamois. He is the father of the doorkeeper Gamal mac Figail, he who was involved in the first set of ritual questions and answers directed at Samildanach (Sections 54 to 66), thus we have here the balance that recurs in all things as we have seen so clearly throughout this legend – the son, Gamal, asked questions of Samildanach, an aspect of Lug; and now the father, Figol, is asked questions by Lug. This balance maintains a link between these oft-times apparently unrelated incidents.

The first thing Figol declares he will do, i.e. rain fire upon the Fomoire, is the first outright magical act using forces not of this world which we have come across so far. The second, however, the binding of urine, is a very earthy act indeed, as have been all the others to date. It was noted earlier in our interpretation of this legend that when whole numbers divisible by three are used it indicates something positive and that when fractions are used it indicates something negative. This can be seen here when Figol says he will rain three showers of fire upon the faces of the Fomorian host – a very positive statement and action – and that he will take out of them two-thirds of their courage, skill at arms and strength – a negative act but one which, hopefully, will have positive results for the Tuatha De Danann.

Section 81

Section 81 sees the end of this series of questions and answers, and by now we should be able to predict that as with everything else in this legend a third series must occur somewhere later in the text. This is indeed the case, but we shall leave a study of this last set of questioning until the appropriate point is reached in the narrative.

This section also lets us know that the name 'the Dagda' means 'the Good God', and is therefore more of a title than a personal name. The motif is exactly the same, albeit on a higher level, as the previous set of questions, being followed as it is by the giving of a title, in the first instance Samildanach and in this instance the Dagda. The Dagda actually repeats Samildanach's declaration, i.e. that he can do all things himself.

It is clear from all this that Sections 78 to 81 are identical in nature and Inner meaning to Sections 55 to 67, if on a different level.

Section 82

Section 82 indicates that this preparatory part of the ritual is now over, and we are returned to this world. The meaning behind 'that day three years later' is again symbolic and is not to be read literally. The three years indicate the three levels, and also is meant to indicate that the passage of time in the Otherworld is different to that of our own, where in fact only one day has elapsed.

Practical Work: Exercise 9

Aengus

Prepare your working area and circle as before and visualize the following scenes as described.

You see before you a little grassy path leading through a thin forest of mature trees. You start to stroll along this path, and as you do so you are aware of the various bird and animal life of the forest. You feel very much at one with them and quite relaxed and happy to be experiencing this pleasant stroll on a warm afternoon.

After a while the trees start to get thicker and thicker and the path becomes more and more overgrown and difficult to make out, until you realize that the path has vanished completely and you are having to push your way through the undergrowth in order to make any progress at all. Suddenly your way is blocked completely by a huge rocky cliff which sprouts up in front of you, making any further progress impossible.

To your left and right the cliff stretches up as far as you can see, and the trees and undergrowth are just as dense as they are in the direction from which you have just come. You stand for a while trying to decide what to do. Whichever way you choose to go is going to be difficult, and even then you do not know where any particular direction may take you. Just when you are beginning to despair you see a couple of white doves flutter out of the undergrowth behind you and settle on the branch of a tree above your head. You hear the noise of twigs being cracked and branches being pushed aside, and realize that someone is coming your way.

A very handsome and trim young man steps into the little clearing where you stand. The doves above you fly down and circle around his head. He smiles at you with an amused expression on his face, and asks if you are lost. You tell him that you are, and that you are not sure which way to go next. He says nothing to this, and you begin to realize that you must ask him very specific questions. He will not volunteer information, and if your question is not clear and precise you will not get a clear nor precise answer, for this is Aengus Mac Oc, the great giver of advice to the Tuatha De Danann and also the great joker and trickster.

It is to Aengus you must turn if you have any problems or queries regarding the best way for you to forge your way in life. We all come to apparently impossible, or unwanted, situations in life, and we all need advice from an impartial observer from time to time in order to make the correct next move. This is Aengus's function, and he will help and advise you.

A word of caution, however: He is not malicious, but his advice often leads you into circumstances which show you very dramatically that most of the awkward and difficult situations you have experienced throughout life were really self-created, and could have been avoided had your earlier actions taken into account any possible later effects they might have had.

Aengus will advise you on the best way to get out of the tangle you presently find yourself in at the foot of the cliff, but I cannot say what his advice will be. He may advise you to climb the cliff, he may tell you to go left or right, or he may tell you to turn back and find the path which you lost earlier in the forest. He may even come up with some other, ingenious solution to this immediate problem. His answer will be different for everyone, but the fact that you do get advice, and it does work for you, shows that you are beginning to be able to handle the experiences these Inner Journeys are designed to throw at you.

As always, once you find your way back to this world close your circle in the proper fashion, put away your Magical Weapons, write up your Magical Diary and have the obligatory snack and drink. Spend some time thinking over your present world situation. Try to see if there are any areas which you are unsure about, or if there are any decisions imminent which it is important for you to get right. These are the sort of things you can ask Aengus (carefully!) about. You should also arrange with him a more convenient place in which to meet him during your future Inner Journeys!

Chapter 11
Sections 83 - 93

The next blocks of the legend to be examined are Sections 83 to 87 and 88 to 93. The first block has unfortunately lost its relevance and therefore its meaning to us today; consequently it appears very obscure and unintelligible to our modern minds. It is included for the sake of completeness and in the hopes that maybe somebody somewhere will be able to get something from it. All I can offer are some general notes and pointers on the passage as a whole.

Sections 83 - 87

83. Then after the preparation for battle had been settled, Lug and the Dagda and Ogma went to the three gods of Danu, and they gave Lug equipment for the battle; and for seven years they had been preparing for them and making their weapons.

    Then she said to him, 'Undertake a battle of overthrowing.' The Morrigan said to Lug, 'Awake . . . . .'

    Then Figol mac Mamois, the druid, was prophesying the battle and strengthening the Tuatha De, saying, 'Battle will be waged . . . .'

84. The Dagda had a house in Glen Edin in the north, and he had arranged to meet a woman in Glen Edin a year from that day, near the All Hallows of the battle. The Unshin of Connacht roars to the south of it.

    He saw the woman at the Unshin of Corann,

washing, with one of her feet at Allod Echae (that is, Aghanagh) south of the water and the other at Lisconny north of the water. There were nine loosened tresses on her head. The Dagda spoke with her, and they united. 'The Bed of the Couple' was the name of that place from that time on. (The woman mentioned here is the Morrigan.)

85. Then she told the Dagda that the Fomoire would land at Mag Ceidne, and that he should summon the aes dana of Ireland to meet her at the ford of Unshin, and she would go into Scetne to destroy Indech mac De Domnann, the king of the Fomoire, and would take from him the blood of his heart and the kidneys of his valour. Later she gave two handfuls of that blood to the hosts that were waiting at the Ford of the Unshin. Its name became 'The Ford of Destruction' because of that destruction of the king.

86. So the aes dana did that, and they chanted spells against the Fomorian host.

87. This was a week before All Hallows, and they all dispersed until all the men of Ireland came together the day before All Hallows. Their number was six times thirty hundred, that is, each third consisted of twice thirty hundred.

It may well be that this very ritualistic sequence of events was relevant to the warrior caste of the day, and that consequently its relevance has been lost to us nowadays. Section 83 in particular seems to contain poetry included specifically to infuse the warriors with courage and bravery, but the language is so obscure that it is impossible to translate the whole section with any certainty of accuracy. There is probably some symbolism contained within the three groups of three deities – Lug, the Dagda and Ogma, the three gods of Danu, and the Morrigan, who was a triple-aspected Goddess of War. The magical period of seven years comes up again, and indeed the whole section has an Otherworldly air about it.

The fact that its full meaning and significance is no longer obvious to us, whereas most of the rest of this same legend is accessible, only serves to show the organic nature of the material we are dealing with. We are no longer a society structured along the same warrior ways as were the Irish Celts, and therefore we do not need the practical information or instruction contained within these obscure passages. It is clear however from passages like these that the ancient Celts did practise a very strict and spiritual as well as physical form of the martial arts, and those readers who are interested in the martial arts may like to study these sections further, as there may well be something of value to be gained by their perusal.

Section 84, by its very wording, reads like a further phase of the magical ritual being acted out for the benefit of the warriors. The date, All Hallows, is very significant, as it is one of the most important of the in-between times which I have mentioned before. Most practitioners of the Celtic system would give this date its non-Christian name of Samhain, the 31st of October in our calendar and for the Celts the end of one year and the beginning of the next. The day itself, or strictly speaking the evening and night of the 31st, were considered to be outside the effects of ordinary time, and it was also a time when this world and the Otherworld converged and passage from one to the other was made easy.

The second paragraph of this section introduces a scene and a character which crop up in Celtic lore to this day throughout the Celtic countries. This character is usually called the Washer of the Ford, and she is always seen, as in this case, washing clothes in a river immediately prior to a battle or, in more modern times, prior to a death in the family. The clothes she washes are usually blood-stained shrouds, and it is a very bad omen indeed for a warrior to meet the Washer of the Ford on his way to battle.

The Washer of the Ford is, in this case, the Morrigan, and her sexual aspect is clearly demonstrated in this section. All the goddesses associated with war were also closely associated with sexuality, and they can be considered both the takers and the givers of life. The Dagda also demonstrates his sexual nature in this section; later in the legend this aspect of his character is repeated, and he too is associated with death as we saw during the incident with Cridenbel, the corrupt satirist (see Section 26, page 105).

I do not know the significance of the location, the

Morrigan straddling the river, her nine loosened tresses or her uniting with the Dagda, but not being able fully to interpret this strange passage does not seem to affect our understanding of the rest of the legend, and therefore I do not propose to attempt to go into these mysteries in any depth.

Sections 88 – 92

The next block of the text, Sections 88 to 92, continues this bizarre episode, and is again set down here only in order to give the reader the complete legend of *The Battle of Moytura* as we have it today. The general impression given in this passage, despite the almost burlesque comedy of the incident described, is that it is none the less important and contains instructions of one sort or another which would have been recognized immediately as being of great relevance to the Irish warriors of early Celtic times.

Whatever it may have meant originally it now means very little to us, and similarly, as is the way of these things, there will be passages which are of great significance to us today which, in the same manner, will lose their relevance and meaning for future generations and will no doubt appear just as odd and as meaningless to them as this passage does to us now. But to keep the legend intact here are the next sections:

88. Then Lug sent the Dagda to spy on the Fomoire and to delay them until the men of Ireland came to the battle.
89. Then the Dagda went to the Fomorian camp and asked them for a truce of battle. This was granted to him as he asked. The Fomoire made porridge for him to mock him, because his love of porridge was great. They filled for him the king's cauldron, which was five fists deep, and poured four score gallons of new milk and the same quantity of meal and fat into it. They put goats and sheep and swine into it, and boiled them all together with the porridge. Then they poured it into a hole in the ground, and Indech said to him that he would be killed unless he consumed it all; he should

eat his fill so that he might not satirize the Fomoire.
90. Then the Dagda took his ladle, and it was big enough for a man and a woman to lie in the middle of it. These are the bits that were in it: halves of salted swine and a quarter of lard.
91. Then the Dagda said, 'This is good food if its broth is equal to its taste.' But when he would put the full ladle into his mouth he said, ' "Its poor bits do not spoil it," says the wise old man.'
92. Then at the end he scraped his bent finger over the bottom of the hole among mould and gravel. He fell asleep then after eating his porridge. His belly was as big as a house cauldron, and the Fomoire laughed at it.

The most obvious piece of symbolism extant in this seemingly pointless passage is the connection made yet again between the Dagda and the cauldron, and also between the Dagda and very earthy and bodily needs and functions. The first mention of the Dagda was in Section 6 (page 23), where we were told that from the city of Murias was brought the Dagda's cauldron, and the first incident actually involving him was in Section 24 (page 105), where we were told he built Bres's fortress and then went on to construct massive earth defences around it. Every time he has been mentioned, therefore, he is associated with either a cauldron or very ordinary, physical functions including manual labour, eating, and sexual activity. He is clearly the deity to cultivate if we wish to further our knowledge of any of these things or, perhaps, if we wish to increase our capabilities in regarding any of these functions. An obvious magical symbol and ritual tool to be used in this context must be the cauldron. The Dagda does also seem to have some sort of a connection with satire and/or satirists.

The way in which this episode opens in Section 88, with Lug instructing the Dagda to go to the Fomorian camp and delay them 'until the men of Ireland came to the battle', indicates that although the necessary forces, stresses and strains have been set in motion on a higher level, the events of the physical world must wait until these magical forces can make themselves available at the physical level. The fact that the Fomoire seem so readily to agree to a pre-battle truce, and use the time for a bit of sport, mocking the Dagda, indicates that they are not as knowledgeable nor as skilled in the workings of the magical forces as are the Tuatha De Danann, else they would have seized the opportunity to attack before the Tuatha De Danann were completely ready.

There may be information contained between the lines of this curious incident concerning pre-battle rest or recreation which would have been aimed at the warriors of the day, but to us nowadays the whole parable seems pointless and irrelevant as far as the rest of the legend is concerned. The fact that this passage was ever included in the legend at all, however, indicates that it is our interpretation of it which is lacking and not the text itself.

Section 93

The next section is the longest so far, and contains more adventures of the Dagda. Again all of these are of a very base nature. It is not clear whether the symbolism contained within this incident was aimed at the warrior caste or not, as, on the surface, it seems to be connected purely with physical functions and sexual satisfaction. There is a link between sex and warfare, as indicated by our brief look at the Morrigan earlier, so this section may well be carrying on the theme of Sections 83 to 85, above.

Whatever its hidden message, its overt meanings are plain enough – indeed, this section could be held up as proof that this legend was not altered by the Christian scribes who set it down. If they had wished to 'clean up' the stories for Christian consumption, as most commentators argue, I find it difficult to believe that they would have left this section in, since it contains very graphic descriptions of bodily functions which even today are not openly discussed; there is as well its erotic content to take into consideration. It is not the sort of material that celibate monks would have considered worthy of preserving had their only intention been to put pre-Christian mythology into an acceptable Christianized form.

The reader can judged for him- or herself, by studying the section in question:

93. Then he went away from them to Traigh Eabha. It was
not easy for the warrior to move along on account of
the size of his belly. His appearance was unsightly: he
had a cape to the hollow of his elbows, and a gray-
brown tunic around him as far as the swelling of his
rump. He trailed behind him a wheeled fork which was
the work of eight men to move, and its track was
enough for the boundary ditch of a province. It is called
'The Track of the Dagda's Club' for that reason. His
long penis was uncovered. He had on two shoes of
horse-hide with the hair outside.

As he went along he saw a girl in front of him, a
good-looking young woman with an excellent figure,
her hair in beautiful tresses. The Dagda desired her,
but he was impotent on account of his belly. The girl
began to mock him, then she began wrestling with
him. She hurled him so that he sank to the hollow of
his rump in the ground. He looked at her angrily and
asked, 'What business did you have, girl, heaving me
out of my right way?'

'This business: to get you to carry me on your back
to my father's house.'

'Who is your father?' he asked.

'I am the daughter of Indech, son of De Domnann,'
she said.

She fell upon him again and beat him hard, so that
the furrow around him filled with the excrement from
his belly; and she satirized him three times so that he
would carry her upon his back.

He said that it was a ges for him to carry anyone who
would not call him by his name.

'What is your name?' she asked.

'Fer Benn,' he said.

'That name is too much!' she said, 'Get up, carry me
on your back, Fer Benn.'

'That is indeed not my name,' he said.

'What is?' she asked.

'Fer Benn Bruach,' he answered.

'Get up, carry me on your back, Fer Benn Bruach,'
she said.

'That is not my name,' he said.

'What is?' she asked. Then he told her the whole

thing. She replied immediately and said, 'Get up, carry me on your back, Fer Benn Bruach Brogaill Broumide Cerbad Caic Rolaig Builc Labair Cerrce Di Brig Oldathair Boith Athgen mBethai Brightere Tri Carboid Roth Rimaire Riog Scotbe Obthe Olaithbe. Get up, carry me away from here!'

'Do not mock me any more, girl,' he said.

'It will certainly be hard,' she said.

Then he moved out of the hole, after letting go the contents of his belly, and the girl had waited for that for a long time. He got up then, and took the girl on his back; and he put three stones in his belt. Each stone fell from it in turn - and it has been said that they were his testicles which fell from it. The girl jumped on him and struck him across the rump, and her curly pubic hair was revealed. Then the Dagda gained a mistress, and they made love. The mark remains at Beltraw Strand where they came together.

Then the girl said to him, 'You will not go to the battle by any means.'

'Certainly I will go,' said the Dagda.

'You will not go,' said the woman, 'because I will be a stone at the mouth of every ford you will cross.'

'That will be true,' said the Dagda, 'but you will not keep me from it. I will tread heavily on every stone, and the trace of my heel will remain on every stone forever.'

'That will be true, but they will be turned over so that you may not see them. You will not go past me until I summon the sons of Tethra from the sid-mounds, because I will be a giant oak in every ford and in every pass you will cross.'

'I will indeed go past,' said the Dagda, 'and the mark of my axe will remain in every oak forever.' (And people have remarked upon the mark of the Dagda's axe.)

Then however she said, 'Allow the Fomoire to enter the land, because the men of Ireland have all come together in one place.' She said that she would hinder the Fomoire, and she would sing spells against them, and she would practise the deadly art of the wand against them - and she alone would take on a ninth part of the host.

This section begins by continuing the account of the totally bizarre antics of the Dagda, and by the description given of him makes him out to be a complete fool. This, however, is actually very significant, for the Fool, as in most mythologies, was a very important person, and usually the one who started off being mocked and ridiculed but who, by the end of the story, saved the day or put forward a sensible, often clever, solution to an apparently insurmountable problem. This is what happens here, for by the end of this section the whole scenario has changed, and the Dagda is clearly very much in charge and able to counter the claims of the Fomorian princess to such an extent that she ends up on his side, agreeing to fight against her own father.

The fact that he left the Fomorian camp and went to a place called Traigh Eabha is significant in itself, as the word 'Traigh' means a beach or shore-line. Beaches and fords are, as has already been said, 'in-between' places, and are therefore magically important and indicative of momentous events about to be described in the text following. The reference to the track left by his massive club may well be a deliberate pun, as the word for club is the same as the word for penis. This is introduced outright in the next sentence, which states 'His long penis was uncovered.'

As in the previous passages, the Dagda is again described as performing very basic bodily functions, and once more shows his great sexual appetite, although in this instance it seems it is the girl who first desires him, despite his grotesque appearance. It is strange that although the girl declares her father to be the Fomorian king Indech mac De Domnann she does not give her own name.

The word 'ges' is usually translated as 'taboo' or 'prohibition', and it was a strange facet of ancient Irish Celtic life. Basically it meant that certain conditions or prohibitions were placed on a person, usually at birth, and it was forbidden for anyone to go against these *gesa*. To do so usually resulted in that person's death by means of the very events or at the hands of the very people they were supposed to avoid. It was also common for the characters in legends such as this one to find themselves trapped in situations where they had no option but to break their own ges and, at that point, accept that their own death would soon befall them.

Clearly one of the Dagda's ges was not to carry anyone upon his back who did not know his name. The introduction of a ges at this point indicates that what is about to follow is going to be of great importance; this can be seen by the structured and formal set of questions and answers carried out between the girl and the Dagda. This questioning is split into three sections: the first time the Dagda gives away a bit of his name, the second time a little bit more, and by the third time he reveals it completely. It is hard to say not only this very lengthy name itself but what it may mean, as the words are so archaic and obscure, but we can hazard a guess at some of them. 'Fer' means 'man', 'Benn' means 'horn' or 'point', 'Bruach' big-bellied, 'Cerbad' to hack off or dismember, 'Caic' excrement, 'Rolaig' warrior, 'Builc' belly, 'Labair' talkative or boastful, 'Di Brig' power or authority, 'Oldathair' great father, 'Athgen mBethai' rebirth of the world, 'Obthe' rejecting, 'Olaithbe' great decay – all names that emphasize the Dagda's very earthy functions. The proliferation of his names also indicates his many associations and attributes and, in a sense, makes him one of the more important deities despite his apparent crudeness and stupidity.

These three naming questions are followed by the Dagda's placing of three stones in his belt – note that the stones are also associated with his sexual aspect, being described as his testicles – this once again obviously must have been of some relevance and importance originally, but to us it is no more than a very odd and apparently garbled succession of incidents.

As with his meeting with the Morrigan in Section 84, this meeting results in the Dagda's coupling with the girl and leaving a physical mark on the land itself. There is always this connection made, between fighting, as the girl has been doing with the Dagda, sexual union, and the resultant physical manifestation on or in the very earth itself.

Clearly much occult lore is jumbled up here and needs sorting out and unravelling in order for us to be able to assess whether it is still of use to us today, but this is a process beyond the scope of this present book.

After the first set of questions and answers, and after their physical uniting, there follows another set of three questions and answers, this time concerning whether the Dagda will be allowed to go to the battle or not. He must have answered these questions correctly, for the result is an apparent complete change of heart on the girl's part, until finally she announces that she will use her deadly magical arts against her father and his invading army. It is important to note here that she refers to 'the men of Ireland', and not to the Tuatha De Danann, as those who are gathering for battle with the Fomoire.

Information regarding specific associations between deities and, for example, weapons, plants, animals or birds, is often given in these legends, as we have already seen. These associated symbols are used as a sort of recognizable icon for those undertaking Otherworld journeys in an attempt to make conscious contact with a specific character or deity. Thus there may well be a connection between the Dagda and the oak tree, for in this section the oak tree is specifically named as opposed to any other type of tree, which would presumably have served the legend's purposes just as well. It is clearly stated that the Dagda literally left his mark on this particular tree. Later in the legend the Dagda recovers his stolen harp which also has a connection with oak. Little bits of information such as this can be very useful when it comes to making sense of the symbolism encountered during Otherworld voyages, and it is worthwhile paying close attention to passages like this one, where the iconography might otherwise be easily missed.

Practical Work: Exercise 10

Airmed

Commence as before with the construction of your basic circle. Then visualize the following scenes.

When your Inner eyes open up you find that it is dusk and you are alone on a bleak, windswept peat moor. There is nothing to see but miles and miles of desolate moor stretching off in all directions. It is cold, and night will soon be upon you. There is no point in simply standing where you are, so you start to walk off through the rough heather beneath your feet, hoping that you will soon find some shelter for the night.

You walk for what seems a very long time. The only change you notice is that it is getting darker and darker. Suddenly through the gloom you are sure that ahead of you, you can make out a faint light against the blackness of the moor. Yes, there is definitely a dim light and you are walking towards it. It appears and disappears as the contours of the ground before you rise and fall, but presently you get close enough to see that it emanates from a tiny cottage with faded white walls and a heather roof held down by great stones on rough heather ropes.

As you approach the rough wooden door you hold your breath in an attempt to hear what is going on inside. There is only the sound of the wind moaning through the heather thatch. You give a little knock and stand back, not knowing what to expect. Nothing happens. You knock again, still nothing. Presently you pluck up courage and give the door a little push. It opens easily and silently and you step warily into the little room. Inside it is warm and there is a lovely orange glow coming from the peat fire right in the centre of the bare earthen floor. There are a couple of wooden stools and an uneven table but no other furniture. You notice, however, that the walls are completely lined with shelves full of bottles of various shapes and sizes containing all sorts of potions, powders, roots, herbs and liquids. None are labelled.

You get quite a start as a door in the far wall suddenly opens and a young woman walks in carrying a dark bottle and a crude wooden cup. She places the bottle back in its proper place on one of the shelves and puts the cup on the table. She sits herself down on one of the stools and motions to you to sit on the other. This is Airmed, one of the great healers of the Tuatha De Danann and an expert in herb-lore and so-called traditional medicines. She can give you advice not only on medical matters but on the exact nature and property of each and every plant, tree, flower and herb. Her advice may not be of great importance to everyone who takes up the Irish Celtic Magical tradition, but those readers interested in herb-lore are advised to make a strong contact with Airmed and to listen carefully to what she has to say.

Once your discussions are over and it is time to close the Inner Journey for this session, step outside the cottage, where you will find it is now dawn. After thanking Airmed for her help and time, close down your Inner senses and make yourself aware of being fully back in this world. Follow this with the now familiar closing-down procedures and write up your Magical Diary as necessary.

Chapter 12
Sections 94 - 121

The narrative from Section 94 returns to the preparations being made for battle by both the Fomoire and the Tuatha De Danann. These sections once again make sense and reveal meaningful information and instruction. The next block to be examined is made up of Sections 94 to 121:

94. The Fomoire advanced until their tenths were in Scetne. The men of Ireland were in Mag Aurfolaig. At this point these two hosts were threatening battle.

    'Do the men of Ireland undertake to give battle to us?' said Bres mac Elathan to Indech mac De Domnann.

    'I will give the same,' said Indech, 'so that their bones will be small if they do not pay their tribute.'

95. In order to protect him, the men of Ireland had agreed to keep Lug from the battle. His nine foster-fathers came to guard him: Tollusdam and Echdam and Eru, Rechtaid Finn and Fosad and Feidlimid, Ibar and Scibar and Minn. They feared an early death for the warrior because of the great number of his arts. For that reason they did not let him go to the battle.

96. Then the men of rank among the Tuatha De were assembled around Lug. He asked his smith, Goibniu, what power he wielded for them.

97. 'Not hard to say,' he said, 'Even if the men of Ireland continue the battle for seven years, for every spear that separates from its shaft or sword that will break in battle, I will provide a new weapon in its place. No

spearpoint which my hand forges will make a missing cast. No skin which it pierces will taste life afterwards. Dolb, the Fomorian smith, cannot do that. I am now concerned with my preparation for the battle of Mag Tuired.'

98. 'And you, Dian Cecht,' said Lug, 'what power do you wield?'

99. 'Not hard to say,' he said, 'Any man who will be wounded there, unless his head is cut off, or the membrane of his brain or his spinal cord is severed, I will make him perfectly whole in the battle on the next day.'

100. 'And you, Credne,' Lug said to his brazier, 'what is your power in the battle?'

101. 'Not hard to answer,' said Credne, 'I will supply them all with rivets for their spears and hilts for their swords and bosses and rims for their shields.'

102. 'And you, Luchta,' Lug said to his carpenter, 'what power would you attain in the battle?'

103. 'Not hard to answer,' said Luchta, 'I will supply them all with whatever shields and spearshafts they need.'

104. 'And you, Ogma,' said Lug to his champion, 'what is your power in the battle?'

105. 'Not hard to say,' he said, 'Being a match for the king and holding my own against twenty-seven of his friends, while winning a third of the battle for the men of Ireland.'

106. 'And you, Morrigan,' said Lug, 'what power?'

107. 'Not hard to say,' she said, 'I have stood fast; I shall pursue what was watched; I will be able to kill; I will be able to destroy those who might be subdued.'

108. 'And you, sorcerers,' said Lug, 'what power?'

109. 'Not hard to say,' said the sorcerers, 'Their white soles will be visible after they have been overthrown by our craft, so that they can easily be killed; and we will take two-thirds of their strength from them, and prevent them from urinating.'

110. 'And you, cupbearers,' said Lug, 'what power?'

111. 'Not hard to say,' said the cupbearers, 'We will bring a great thirst upon them, and they will not find drink to quench it.'

112. 'And you, druids,' said Lug, 'what power?'

113. 'Not hard to say,' said the druids, 'We will bring showers of fire upon the faces of the Fomoire so that they cannot look up, and the warriors contending with them can use their force to kill them.'

114. 'And you, Coirpre mac Etaine,' said Lug to his poet, 'what can you do in the battle?'

115. 'Not hard to say,' said Coirpre, 'I will make a glam dicenn against them, and I will satirize them and shame them so that through the spell of my art they will offer no resistance to warriors.'

116. 'And you, Be Chuille and Dianann,' said Lug to his two witches, 'what can you do in the battle?'

117. 'Not hard to say,' they said, 'We will enchant the trees and the stones and the sods of the earth so that they will be a host under arms against them; and they will scatter in flight terrified and trembling.'

118. 'And you, Dagda,' said Lug, 'what power can you wield against the Fomorian host in battle?'

119. 'Not hard to say,' said the Dagda, 'I will fight for the men of Ireland with mutual smiting and destruction and wizardry. Their bones under my club will soon be as many as hailstones under the feet of herds of horses where the double enemy meets on the battlefield of Mag Tuired.'

120. Then in this way Lug addressed each of them in turn concerning their arts, strengthening them and addressing them in such a way that every man had the courage of a king or great lord.

121. Now every day the battle was drawn up between the race of the Fomoire and the Tuatha De Danann, but there were no kings or princes waging it, only fierce and arrogant men.

Section 94

The location given in Section 94, Scetne, is significant, as this is the same place where the original invaders of Ireland, under the leadership of Cessair, according to legend first landed and settled on Irish soil. The importance of this is that it indicates that the forthcoming battle is going to be as momentous an affair as the first-ever invasion of Ireland. Considering that Ireland represents the physical world, this then is a conflict that will affect all of us.

It is also important to note that the text says, 'The men of Ireland' were in Mag Aurfolaig, and not that the Tuatha De Danann were at this location. Bres then asks the question, 'Do the men of Ireland undertake to give battle to us?', which shows that even he is surprised to see them, for where are his main opponents, the Tuatha De Danann? The answer is that they are still making magical preparations for this crucial battle in the Otherworld and, as in any magical ritual or operation, they need a physical link in order to make real in this world their Otherworld creations. The physical-level men of Ireland are this necessary link. Bres, who is clearly not versed in the magical arts, does not understand this subtle point; hence his rather naïve question.

It is Indech mac De Domnann to whom Bres is talking, and he who replies in very valiant tones and declares his intention to crush this uprising. He is a character who has cropped up from time to time before in this legend, and he is quite an important character. In the rather baffling events described in Section 85, for example, it will be noted that the Morrigan announced she would kill Indech and use his blood and kidneys in some sort of ritualistic way. In the sections that follow we see that despite all the magnificent claims put forward by the individual members of the Tuatha De Danann when questioned by Lug, it is only the Morrigan who actually claims she will be able to kill. All of the others play supporting roles to the men of Ireland, that is, the ones doing the actual killing, but the Morrigan, the Goddess of War, is the only one who says she will do battle herself.

Section 95

Section 95 shows that although the men of Ireland may be excellent warriors and champions of their arts, they do not know much about the ways of magic, or they would not have attempted to stop Lug from going to the battle. This shows that when working with magical forces, and especially ones with a strong Earth contact, you must be very careful to ensure that everything goes the way you intend it to, do not leave anything to chance or, indeed, for others to do on your behalf.

The number of Lug's foster-fathers is obviously symbolic, and their names were no doubt of some relevance at one time. For us today, however, their names are so archaic that it is not clear what they mean. It would also seem that Lug has taken on the role of the king, for if he were still simply a warrior then there would have been no question about keeping him away from the battle, quite the opposite in fact. The reason he is being kept from the battle, and therefore the possibility of death, is that he is now the king, either symbolically or actually, and if he were to fall in battle it would spell defeat for all of the men of Ireland and all of the Tuatha De Danann.

Sections 96 – 119

Section 96 begins the third and final set of ritualistic questions and answers. It will be noted that the first set (Sections 56 – 67) was directed at Samildanach, the mental aspect of Lug, on his arrival at Tara. In this third set it is now Lug who is the questioner and all the individual craftsmen of the Tuatha De Danann who are the respondents. This is the necessary reversal, or Polar opposite, of the first set of questions, and shows that all is in balance and obeying the cosmic law of Polarity and its constant switching from one Pole to the other.

This final set of questions and answers involves nearly all of the characters who were named during the first questioning; most of them have retained their original functions or crafts. The first question is directed at the smith Goibniu, who asserts that he will make good any weapons damaged during the conflict, and adds that the Fomorian smith is unable to do this. The symbolic period of seven years is mentioned again, and we can infer from this and from Goibniu's declaration generally that his power of smithcraft is actually wielded on a magical level and not so much on the purely physical level. This of course can be considered in the reverse fashion, so that it becomes clear that all physical crafts or skills must have a higher or magical aspect to them. To become a master craftsman, in any craft, it is necessary to be able to work your craft on all of its levels.

The second question, in Section 98, is directed at the physician Dian Cecht. It is met with a very positive statement of ability, also very magical in nature. It is interesting to note that Dian Cecht declares he can heal any injury other than those of the head or spinal cord. This has already been demonstrated in Section 34, when Dian Cecht's own son Miach was able to heal himself of the injuries inflicted upon him by his father until his father struck him so hard that the membrane of his brain was damaged, and he died since this injury he could not cure.

This section and those dealing with the Dagda are a bit disturbing to us today because both of these characters are murderers. The Dagda deliberately killed the satirist Cridenbel and Dian Cecht murdered his own son in cold blood. Neither of them were punished in any way, however, and are still very much at the forefront of what is going on as regards the battle and very much in favour not only with Lug but with the rest of the Tuatha De Danann as well.

It is important to note this point because it demonstrates one of the great differences between what is acceptable in this world and what is acceptable in the Otherworld. It has been stressed all along that journeying to the Otherworld in order to experience it and meet its inhabitants first hand is possible, but it has also been stressed that the Otherworld and its inhabitants should not be looked upon as being simply another facet or some kind of an extension of this world. Things are very different there, and one of the more disturbing differences is this apparent lack of retribution.

The whole concept of reward or punishment for words or actions is alien to the Irish system, and this takes a bit of getting used to for those of us brought up under the way of life of a Western Christian society. With a bit of thought, though, it is not hard to see that a great deal of our sense of justice, or of right and wrong, is really only based on value judgements, usually personal ones, and it must be realized that in the Otherworld the personality, as we understand it, does not exist, and therefore the laws of that world are based on very different value judgements indeed.

The next two questions, directed at the brazier Credne and the carpenter Luchta respectively, meet with the same answers that Goibniu gave; they will repair the broken weapons of the men of Ireland and make them ready for use in battle the following day. This seems to imply some sort of magical recycling ability on the part of the Tuatha De Danann, and this indeed is one of the most basic functions of magic even today – to repair or re-use something which has been damaged rather than try to create something new altogether.

This is merely a continuation of the same principle in use all the time on the physical level, particularly in the spheres of medicine and psychiatry. We do not attempt to make something new when we are ill physically or mentally, instead we try to repair what is already there and make it whole and useful again. This principle should be applied to everything and every situation wherever possible.

Ogma the champion gives the sort of reply we would expect from a champion, declaring his great feats of strength and fighting ability. Morrigan is, as I said above, the only character so far, and indeed for the rest of this series of questions, who claims she will actually kill enemy warriors. All of the rest of the Tuatha De Danann declare support roles for the men of Ireland as opposed to getting personally or actively involved in the fray; the Morrigan is the only one who states specifically 'I will be able to kill; I will be able to destroy'. This reveals a few important pointers for those of us studying the Irish magical system today.

First, the most important thing to note is that the Morrigan, being a Goddess of War, is not the sort of Otherworld character you would want to attempt to contact if all you fancy is a bit of a chat and a giggle. She is a very fearsome deity, and should be treated with the utmost respect if you should be unfortunate enough to encounter her. Keeping in mind what was said above about different value judgements between this world and the Otherworld, it should be realized that the Morrigan who is 'able to kill' does not care for the status, ability or purpose of the individual. Her function is to kill and destroy, usually through war, and as such she should be avoided as far as is possible, for the sort of powers she possesses are not ones we would want to employ or even witness.

The rest of Lug's questions are directed at the practitioners of the magical arts among the Tuatha De Danann – the sorcerers, cupbearers, druids, the poet and the two witches. All of them reply that they will assist the men of Ireland in various magical ways, all of which are similar to those already stated in the second set of questions and answers (Sections 78 - 81). Once again we see that the magical powers of these skilled magicians rely heavily on the ordinary energies and forces of the Earth for support; they are not some vague or totally mysterious manifestations as we tend nowadays to associate with 'magical powers'.

Lug's final question is addressed to the Dagda, who likewise claims he will give support to the men of Ireland both with his own strength and with his magical ability. The rather formal-sounding last sentence, ending with, 'where the double enemy meets on the battlefield of Mag Tuired' is very similar to the last part of the answer given by Goibniu in Section 97 when he says, 'I am now concerned with my preparation for the battle of Mag Tuired.' This similarity is deliberate, and indicates the beginning and ending respectively of the formal question and answer set, which is an important part of ritual and copies the style of Bardic poetry (true Bardic poems started and finished on the same word or phrase).

All of this formality and the specific naming of people, functions and abilities may seem irrelevant to those of us wishing to study and practise the ancient Irish Celtic system of magic, but it does serve to reveal an important aspect of any magical ritual, modern or ancient, which is sometimes overlooked by those organizing the ritual. It is vitally important for each participant in such a magical working to know exactly what his or her individual capabilities are and exactly what role or function is to be pursued during the work about to be undertaken. To omit this defining of people/powers/functions at the outset can lead to sloppy practices at best and total confusion, resulting in a failed ritual or emotionally upset and confused individuals, at worst.

In this case Lug seeks to identify and clarify who can do what to benefit the men of Ireland and, ultimately, the Tuatha De Danann as well. From the replies he receives he is satisfied that he has the people he needs to undertake the work in hand, and that these individuals are capable of carrying it through successfully. Remember this in any work you intend to carry out. Check carefully those assisting you (assuming you have already satisfied yourself of your own ability of course), and if there is a weakness or even a doubt as to the correct number of people involved or their own capability and reliability, then the work should be abandoned before it even begins. Powerful forces are brought into play during any magical working no matter its physical-level purpose or intended outcome, and you cannot afford to take risks with these forces any more than you can when dealing with such things as electricity or gas.

Practical Work: Exercise 11

Free-form

By now you should be familiar with the general principles behind these Inner Journeys, and should realize the way in which the various symbols and scenes have been developed around each of the specific Otherworld beings mentioned so far. If you spent sufficient time in the first four exercises with the Four Teachers of the Tuatha De Danann you should now be capable of making your own Inner imagery and Inner Journeys in order to contact those other members of the Tuatha De Danann named and identified in the text of *The Battle of Moytura*.

You should now spend some time formulating new contacts, with the help of your guide and friend whom you met in the first exercise, and start to become familiar not only with the layout of the Otherworld as it appears to you but also with the beings who live there and what they have to offer you. Remember of course that you may be asked to do something for them on this level in return for the information provided by them at their level. This is quite acceptable and is a vital part of the all-important principle of bringing things that originate in the Otherworld through to this world.

Enough information and hints have been given in the notes to this legend to make these Journeys and exchanges possible, and it could be said that this in itself is a lifetime's work. It is important, however, to keep yourself and your magical work well anchored in this world; the rest of the Practical Work will concentrate on so doing. For the time being, however, familiarize yourself with your own Inner territory, make new contacts, and most important, keep detailed records of all that you see, do and encounter. It is from such notes that real gems of enlightenment can be gleaned, maybe even years from now, when your understanding will have developed even further.

Chapter 13
Sections 122 - 126

The next block of text for us to examine describes the start of the battle proper:

122. One thing which became evident to the Fomoire in the battle seemed remarkable to them. Their weapons, their spears and their swords, were blunted; and those of their men who were killed did not come back the next day. That was not the case with the Tuatha De Danann: although their weapons were blunted one day, they were restored the next because Goibniu the smith was in the smithy making swords and spears and javelins. He would make those weapons with three strokes. Then Luchta the carpenter would make the spearshafts in three chippings, and the third chipping was a finish and would set them in the socket of the spear. After the spearheads were in the side of the forge he would throw the sockets with the shafts, and it was not necessary to set them again. Then Credne the brazier would make the rivets with three strokes, and he would throw the sockets of the spears at them, and it was not necessary to drill holes for them; and they stayed together this way.

123. Now this is what used to kindle the warriors who were wounded there so that they were more fiery the next day: Dian Cecht, his two sons Octriuil and Miach, and his daughter Airmed were chanting spells over the well named Slaine. They would cast their

mortally-wounded men into it as they were struck
down; and they were alive when they came out. Their
mortally-wounded were healed through the power of
the incantation made by the four physicians who
were around the well.

124. Now that was damaging to the Fomoire, and they
picked a man to reconnoitre the battle and the
practices of the Tuatha De – Ruadan, the son of Bres
and of Brig, the daughter of the Dagda – because he
was a son and a grandson of the Tuatha De. Then he
described to the Fomoire the work of the smith and
the carpenter and the brazier and the four physicians
who were around the well. They sent him back to kill
one of the aes dana, Goibniu. He requested a
spearpoint from him, its rivets from the brazier, and
its shaft from the carpenter; and everything was given
to him as he asked. Now there was a woman there
grinding weapons, Cron the mother of Fianlach; and
she ground Ruadan's spear. So the spear was given to
Ruadan by his maternal kin, and for that reason a
weaver's beam is still called 'the spear of the maternal
kin' in Ireland.

125. But after the spear had been given to him, Ruadan
turned and wounded Goibniu. He pulled out the
spear and hurled it at Ruadan so that it went through
him; and he died in his father's presence in the
Fomorian assembly. Brig came and keened for her
son. At first she shrieked, in the end she wept. Then
for the first time weeping and shrieking were heard
in Ireland. (Now she is the Brig who invented a
whistle for signalling at night.)

126. Then Goibniu went into the well and he became
whole. The Fomoire had a warrior named Ochtriallach,
the son of the Fomorian king Indech mac De
Domnann. He suggested that every single man they
had should bring a stone from the stones of the River
Drowes to cast into the well Slaine in Achad Abla to
the west of Mag Tuired, to the east of Lough Arrow.
They went, and every man put a stone into the well.
For that reason the cairn is called Ochtriallach's Cairn.
But another name for that well is Loch Luibe, because
Dian Cecht put into it every herb that grew in Ireland.

Figure 4:
The Well of Slaine

Section 122

Section 122 indicates that the battle is now in full swing and that a great many men on both sides are involved. It should be kept in mind here that it is the men of Ireland who are fighting the Fomoire on the physical level with the help of the Tuatha De Danann, who are assisting them from the Otherworld, or magical level if you prefer. This is demonstrated clearly by the frequent use of the number three – in the lists of 'weapons, spears and swords' and 'swords, spears and javelins', in the mention of the three craftsmen Goibniu, Luchta and Credne, who gave 'three strokes', 'three chippings' and 'three strokes' respectively.

The Fomoire find it remarkable that the dead warriors of the men of Ireland returned to continue fighting the next day and that their weapons never seemed to become blunt. The Fomoire were not versed in the magical arts, and could only see and understand things from their own very limited level of understanding. This reiterates what has already been said about the dwellers of this world and the dwellers of the Otherworld not being all-knowing. One must learn from the other.

Section 123

Section 123 contains a few things which at first sight may seem puzzling or contradictory. The most obvious anomaly, or apparent anomaly, is that Miach, who was murdered by Dian Cecht in Section 34, is now apparently alive and well and assisting his father, brother and sister in reanimating the dead warriors. In fact there is no anomaly or inconsistency, because the events being described in this section are happening in the Otherworld, whereas the events in Section 34 were happening in this world. When Miach was killed in this world he automatically became 'alive', or shifted his full being and awareness to the Otherworld, where he is now operating and helping in the events taking place back in this world.

This is important, as well as encapsulating a very optimistic message, as it obviously means that as far as the Irish system is concerned it is perfectly feasible to die in this world, go to the Otherworld and, from there, be involved in the events and goings-on of this world. It also shows that those of us still bound to this world can journey to the Otherworld, and there likewise assist and help the inhabitants of the Otherworld in whatever magical work they may be undertaking. This belief in the continuation of life after physical death, and the ability of the 'dead' still to have communion with the living, was so strong it was even reflected in the Brehon Laws, which states that it was permissible to give a loan on the strength of repayment being completed in the Otherworld should the borrower die before repayment was made in full in this one.

The warriors who are reanimated by these four Otherworld physicians, though 'dead' as far as this world is concerned, continue to operate on the physical level in a magical way. Other versions of this legend say that the warriors who returned to do battle after having been killed were unable to speak. This was because the voice, or breath, of the warrior was believed to emanate from his spiritual aspect, a very common theme among the world's many religions and magical systems, and therefore because the spiritual aspect was no longer encapsulated within the physical body, the warrior's voice disappears.

The name of the well, Slaine, is very apt as it means 'entireness, fullness, soundness, completeness and health'. The other name it is given, Loch Luibe (in Section 126) is equally apt, as Luibe means 'herb or plant'. It should be noted from Section 123, however, that it is not the waters of the well itself which are said to cure the warriors, but that 'Their mortally-wounded were healed through the power of the incantation made by the four physicians'. In other words, the well was used as a magical tool but the real power was supplied by the incantations of the magicians practising around it.

Wells are in most countries and traditions considered to be holy and magical, and the Irish system is no exception. Archaeologists have noted the frequency with which human heads have been found at the bottom of wells, the reason behind this being that the well-shaft was seen as a birth-passage from the very depths of the great Mother Earth herself through to this world. What more appropriate magical tool for a ritual involving an easy birth from one level to the other than a well?

This section is the only section which mentions Dian Cecht's son Octriuil, and we know nothing about him. His name may be composed of the words for 'eight', 'month' and some other word or words, but its true meaning is unclear. Airmed, Dian Cecht's daughter, was introduced in Section 35, where she possessed the quickness of thought to spread out the three hundred and sixty-five healing herbs that grew from Miach's grave on her cloak. In that section Dian Cecht's inability to cope with the emotions of this world, especially jealousy, resulted in the true property of each herb being lost forever. Here on the Otherworld level Dian Cecht seems to be in better control of himself, and in Section 126 he tries to make amends for his indiscretion about the herbs by putting them all into the healing well of Slaine; hence its change of name at that point to Loch Luibe, the Loch of Herbs.

Section 124

In Section 124 we note that there are two reasons given for the choice of Ruadan as the Fomorian spy: first, he would have been inconspicuous and able to blend in among the Tuatha De Danann craftsmen as he was part Tuatha De Danann himself, and second, for this same reason he would have been well-equipped to travel to the Otherworld and cope with being there.

His parents and grandparent are all very important characters in the legend, and Brig, or Brigit as she is more usually called, is an extremely important deity indeed, although in this legend this is the only passage in which she makes an appearance. Like all of the other deities of the Tuatha De Danann pantheon she is associated with a specific art or craft, in this case poetry, smithcraft and healing – all of which have been heavily emphasized as playing major roles in the battle so far.

Ruadan, being the offspring of such a powerful Tuatha De Danann line and such an unfortunate Fomorian line, seems to have inherited the qualities of both, in that his Tuatha De Danann side has helped him arrive successfully in the Otherworld to encounter Goibniu, while in his reason for being there at all, deceit, his Fomorian side shines through and he fails, as do all Fomorian actions, it would seem. Ruadan can perhaps be seen as personifying the state most people are in today – they have a strong Tuatha De Danann, or spiritual, side to their natures, but more often than not this is tempered or even over-shadowed by their Fomorian side, which puts self-interest first, and usually pays the price for it!

The reference at the end of this section to the 'weaver's beam' is obscure, and we no longer know why it is introduced at this point. It obviously meant something when the legend was first developed, but its significance is no longer apparent today. This should not however detract from our enjoyment or understanding of the legend in any way.

Section 125

In Section 125 we read that Ruadan attempts to kill Goibniu with the spear he had been given by him but that Goibniu simply pulls it out and throws it back, killing Ruadan instead. Note that Ruadan has to resort to using, or attempting to use, one of the Tuatha De Danann's own weapons. The Fomorian weapons, which are of this world, would have been of no use in the Otherworld.

As soon as this Otherworld weapon delivers its deadly blow to Ruadan he is thrown back into this world, where he physically dies in the Fomorian camp. This demonstrates an important principle, that injuries received while in the Otherworld can 'cross over' and result in an equivalent injury being suffered in this world. It is important to realize this point and therefore to take as many precautions and as much care of yourself in the Otherworld as you would naturally do in this one.

The more you learn of this Irish magical system the more you will realize that it is very far from the pleasant, picturesque mental fantasies that some people seem to think it is. Fortunately those who approach it with a twee, naïve attitude such as this will probably find it exactly as they expected it to be, as they will never be able to make any real progress within this system due to their completely incorrect mental and spiritual attitude. Those who approach it with an open mind and spirit, however, will make real progress, and will soon realize that such progress can be difficult and painful. In many ways there is very little difference between the Otherworld and this world.

The comment at the end of Section 125 about Brig's keening for her son shows that what we would now call human emotions have become manifest in this world. It was noted earlier that the Dagda and Dian Cecht were not punished for committing murder, and that nobody seemed particularly upset by the death of Cridenbel or Miach, and this, as was commented on, was because the value judgements of this world, based as they are on emotions, are very different to those of the Otherworld. Here, though, the response to Ruadan's death is exactly what we would expect from a mother who has lost her son. This shows that the great battle of Mag Tuired, which is still raging all around, is driving a great wedge between the two worlds, which previously had been very close to each other. The eventual result is that this world becomes the world we know today.

The final comment in this section, about Brig inventing a whistle for signalling at night, is as obscure as is the final comment in the previous section about the weaver's beam. It was no doubt inserted to add a bit of weight to Brig's otherwise almost insignificant role in this legend, and may well have had some practical meaning to warriors of the day who, presumably, had some sort of communication system based on different whistles for contacting each other during the hours of darkness.

Section 126

After being skewered by Ruadan's spear-throw, here Goibniu simply dips himself into the Well of Slaine and makes himself whole again. Indech mac De Domnann's son Ochtriallach comes up with an extremely simple but effective solution for destroying the powers of this magical well. Earlier in the legend we noted that second- and subsequent generation Tuatha De Danann were the ones who more often than not came up with solutions to the problems their parents were facing. Here the same scenario is played out, only this time among the Fomorian host.

The way the Fomoire seem to have been able to cast their stones into the waters of the well without any resistance from the Tuatha De Danann, who after all were supposed to be using the well and were presumably camped around it, shows that the Fomoire were attacking the physical-level manifestation of the well whereas the Tuatha De Danann were using it on a different level. Despite this, blocking up the well with stones does seem to put an end to its useful magical properties, although it should be noted that the text does not actually say this. It can be inferred, however, from the fact that the well is not mentioned again, nor is there any further reference made to warriors being brought back to life.

An important point about magic is being revealed here which is similar to the principle demonstrated at the beginning of this legend when we noted that the physical level can very often put up a strong and effective resistance to the wishes and powers of the other levels. What has happened in this incident is that the physical level, using the very substance of that level, i.e. the stones used to block the well, has successfully stopped a very potent manifestation of Otherworld magical power. Clearly this means that the trainee magician must not only concentrate on learning and handling Otherworld powers but must also become familiar with the powers of this world as well. It also shows that it is an error to regard one level as being more powerful or superior to the other. Each has its time, place and function, and if there is a power of this world suited to the task in hand then that is the one to use. Do not automatically look to the Otherworld for solutions to each and every problem.

Practical Work: Exercise 12

The Basic Ritual

The Practical Work now takes a more pragmatic turn, and

will concentrate on the ritualistic nature of magical working.

All magic is based upon patterns, and the basic pattern of the quartered-circle is the fundamental design of all native Western magic. It is therefore on this basis that we shall start to build.

Go to your special place or room, taking with you your four Magical Weapons, four little candles (the 'night-light' type are ideal), a taper and some matches. Spend a moment or two relaxing, controlling and stilling your breathing and quietly contemplating the work you are about to undertake. Place your Weapons, candles, matches and taper in the centre of your working area – trace out the perimeter of the area in the usual way, but be extra aware of forming the circle as clearly and as vividly in your mind as you can. As you go round clockwise, drawing your sword along to mark the circle's circumference, also be aware of your thought processes lifting to a higher level, and of your spiritual aspect awakening and opening up to your conscious mind.

Once your circle has been drawn return to the centre, place your sword on the ground and take up one of the candles. Take it slowly, unlit, to the northern quarter of the circle. As you carry it be aware of the fact that you have become a Light Bearer (at least potentially, for the light has not yet been lit). As you set the candle on the ground just touching the inside of the circumference of your circle, realize that you have just brought the potential for Light to a quarter of all that exists (which is what your circle symbolizes).

Return to the centre, take the next candle, and go to the eastern quarter, keeping the same thoughts in mind. Repeat this process for the southern and western quarters.

Return to the centre, take up your stone and go to the northern quarter. As you do so realize that just as you brought the potential for Light to that quarter, now you are bringing the potential for Energy and Power to that same place. Before setting the stone on the ground in front of the unlit candle, say a few appropriate words, either within yourself or audibly, which express to you the purpose behind the physical act you are presently carrying out. There is no need for me to suggest words, as whatever

you say will be individual and unique to you for that
important moment in time.

Return to the centre, take up your sword, go to the
eastern quarter and repeat the process. Do the same with
your wand in the south and then your cup in the west,
constantly keeping in mind the tremendous potential
behind the creative act you are taking upon yourself.

Once all the Weapons are in place, go to the centre, light
your taper and carry the flame carefully to the candle in
the north. This is a very important part of the ritual, for
as well as being the third act, it transforms you at that
moment into a Light Bearer, with all of the tremendous
symbolism and significance being such a mighty figure
implies. Carefully and slowly light the candle in the
north; as you do so be aware of the little flame of the
candle burning brighter and brighter until the whole of
the northern quarter, on all three levels, is illuminated
with brilliant white light.

Carry the taper round the circumference of the circle to
the candle in the east. As you do so see in your mind's eye
a band of flame extending from the northern candle to the
eastern one. Light this candle, then, with the same
attendant visualization, carry the taper to the south,
seeing the band of flame forming the next part of the
circle, and so on until all four candles are lit and all the
quarters are ablaze with light. Remember to take the taper
back to the northern quarter before returning to the centre
in order to complete the band of flame around the
circumference of your circle.

On your return to the centre of your circle extinguish
the taper and visualize the band of flame around you
starting to rotate in a clockwise direction. As it does so
this band starts to spiral upwards until it forms a great
cone of fire above you, meeting at some point high above
your head. Now visualize the band of flame around you
at your feet starting to spiral anti-clockwise and move
down below you into the very heart of the earth, again
closing in on itself to form a cone extending deep below
you.

As you stand, or sit, within this circle and cone of fire,
realize that you are the centre of the Universe and that
everything, at that moment, rotates around you. The cone

extends into the highest Heavens and meets the stars and also extends below you to meet the very heart of the planet. The point where these two extremes meet and change over is within you. Think upon the significance of all this and realize that by the simple act of forming the circle and opening the quarters you have put yourself in alignment with the greatest of cosmic and terrestrial forces.

You may find at this stage that your guide comes to you with some information or advice. This may not happen, however, and should not be forced if it does not. Simply go with the feel of the moment and take it as it comes. You will probably find, during this time of contemplation, that your sense of ordinary time has left you completely, but having said that, do not over-do this exercise simply for the sake of it. There will come a point when it will feel right naturally to close. Once that point is reached then you should close down the working and not prolong it unnecessarily.

To close the working completely you should visualize the cone of fire shrinking in both directions until it is simply a band of fire hovering above the circumference of your circle. Extinguish the candles in the quarters, starting at the north and going from there to the west, south and east, at the same time visualizing the band of flame disappearing at each quarter until it has gone completely. Return each candle as it is extinguished to the centre before going on to the next one.

Next collect your Magical Weapons, in the same order, and as you take each one from its quarter say appropriate words of thanks to the powers of that quarter, and visualize the link between the three levels being parted. Finally, close the circle in the usual manner by tracing its perimeter anti-clockwise with your sword. Write up your Magical Diary and eat and drink something hot in order fully to close down your psychic centres, which will have been well and truly opened by this exercise.

Chapter 14
Sections 127 - 161

Sections 127 - 132

The next block of text we will examine consists of Sections 127 to 132, which give an account of the battle itself. This battle, it must be remembered, was a very important part of the legend to its Celtic audience, although from our modern perspective its full relevance and appeal is greatly diminished. It is for this same reason that much of the narrative, especially the direct speech, is impossible for us to translate today, as it deals with matters no longer of any practical use to us and based upon thought processes now quite alien to the modern mind.

127. Now when the time came for the great battle, the Fomoire marched out of their encampment and formed themselves into strong indestructible battalions. There was not a chief nor a skilled warrior among them without armour against his skin, a helmet on his head, a broad spear in his right hand, a heavy sharp sword on his belt, a strong shield on his shoulder. To attack the Fomorian host that day was 'striking a head against a cliff,' was 'a hand in a serpent's nest,' was 'a face brought close to fire.'

128. These were the kings and leaders who were encouraging the Fomorian host: Balor son of Dot son of Net, Bres mac Elathan, Tuire Tortbuillech mac Lobois, Goll and Irgoll, Loscennlomm mac Lommgluinigh, Indech mac De Domnann, king of

the Fomoire, Ochtriallach mac Indich, Omna and Bagna, Elatha mac Delbaith.

129. On the other side, the Tuatha De Danann arose and left the nine companions guarding Lug, and went to join the battle. But when the battle ensued, Lug escaped from the guard set over him, as a chariot-fighter, and it was he who was in the front of the battalion of the Tuatha De. Then a keen and cruel battle was fought between the race of the Fomoire and the men of Ireland.

Lug was urging the men of Ireland to fight the battle fiercely so they should not be in bondage any longer, because it was better for them to find death while protecting their fatherland than to be in bondage and under tribute as they had been. Then Lug chanted the spell which follows, going around the men of Ireland on one foot and with one eye closed . . .

130. The hosts gave a great shout as they went into battle. Then they came together, and each of them began to strike the other.

131. Many beautiful men fell there in the stall of death. Great was the slaughter and the grave-lying which took place there. Pride and shame were there side by side. There was anger and indignation. Abundant was the stream of blood over the white skin of young warriors mangled by the hands of bold men while rushing into danger for shame. Harsh was the noise made by the multitude of warriors and champions protecting their swords and shields and bodies while others were striking them with spears and swords. Harsh too the tumult all over the battlefield – the shouting of the warriors and the clashing of bright shields, the swish of swords and ivory-hilted blades, the clatter and rattling of the quivers, the hum and whirr of spears and javelins, the crashing strokes of weapons.

132. As they hacked at each other their fingertips and their feet almost met; and because of the slipperiness of the blood under the warriors' feet, they kept falling down, and their heads were cut off them as they sat. A gory, wound-inflicting, sharp, bloody battle was

upheaved, and spearshafts were reddened in the
hands of foes.

This part of the legend, the description of the great battle
itself, was clearly aimed at pleasing the warrior instincts
of the ancient Irish listener, whereas for our purposes it
contains very little information still relevant or valid today.

This does not lessen its importance in any way, however,
for it should be remembered that this legend was
composed by and for a warrior race, and must therefore
naturally contain passages relating specifically to the
actions of such a people. Like everything else, the legend
as a whole exists on three levels, and this present passage
can be considered as having more relevance on the purely
physical level than on the other two. It is, in essence, the
part of the story intended for those who were only
interested in understanding the legend on a superficial
level only.

From Section 127 onwards there are many sections that
contain text that is so archaic and obscure that it really
is impossible to translate at all. Most of these passages
consist of direct speech; it is probable that they contain
within them the magical aspect of the Craft of the Warrior
specifically, just as the rest of the text contains the
magical aspect of our day-to-day life generally. As we in the
West have forgotten or lost the physical aspect of the
warrior's craft (unlike in the East where the warrior craft,
or the so-called martial arts, are still practised and
flourish), it is not surprising that we can no longer
recognize and understand the higher aspects of this craft.

There is much scope for a deep study of these strange
sections on the part of those who have a natural
inclination towards the very physical side of the ancient
Celtic Craft of the Warrior. This is beyond the scope of this
present work, however, but I give you the text as fully as
possible not only in order to maintain the completeness
of the legend as we have inherited it today but also in the
hopes that some of you may be able to pick up on further
points which have missed my attention, particularly with
regard to the magical aspect of the warrior craft.

Section 129 contains a couple of interesting points
worth comment. In this section we read that Lug escapes

the guard set around him and goes to join the battle. He does not however immediately get involved in the physical, hand-to hand fighting. Instead he starts to incite the men of Ireland to even fiercer fighting by chanting some sort of magical spell. Unfortunately this is one of the passages where we are unable to translate exactly what he says, but the peculiar stance he adopts while reciting his words – on one foot and with one eye closed – is one that occurs frequently in these legends, and always in connection with some magical recitation or other.

The exact purpose behind this is not clear and does not correspond to any known modern-day magical ritual stance or action. It could be a symbolic way of showing that only one side of the natural order of Polarity is being invoked, and this certainly would have very marked physical-level results. Alternatively it could be a poetic way of saying that only one side of Lug was visible as he walked around the men of Ireland, to whom these magical verses were directed. We are told in Section 129 that Lug was indeed 'going around the men of Ireland'. As we know, walking in circles, both clockwise and anti-clockwise, is still an important part of nearly all magical rituals.

This section again hints at the fact that Lug is now at least symbolically the king; below we shall see this idea further elaborated in Section 133, where although Nuadu is killed the Tuatha De Danann and the men of Ireland fight on. If Nuadu was at that point still the king then the battle would have come to an immediate halt at the time of his death. The fact that it doesn't, and that Lug seems to take up the main action from then on, indicates that we should now consider Lug to be the king of the Tuatha De Danann even though the text never specifically tells us this.

Sections 130 to 132 serve the same purpose as do the previous eight sections, i.e. to satisfy the blood-lust of the ancient listener to this legend of war and warriors – which is, after all, at least on the surface, what the whole story is all about.

Sections 133 – 138

Sections 133 to 138 continue the bloody description of

this very fierce and gory battle, and tell us the fate of some of the key characters, as follows:

133. Then Nuadu Silverhand and Macha the daughter of Ernmas fell at the hands of Balor grandson of Net. Casmael fell at the hands of Ochtriallach son of Indech. Lug and Balor of the piercing eye met in the battle. The latter had a destructive eye which was never opened except on a battlefield. Four men would raise the lid of the eye by a polished ring in its lid. The host which looked at that eye, even if they were many thousands in number, would offer no resistance to warriors. It had that poisonous power for this reason: once his father's druids were brewing magic. He came and looked over the window, and the fumes of the concoction affected the eye and the venomous power of the brew settled in it. Then he and Lug met . . .

134. 'Lift up my eyelid, lad,' said Balor, 'so I may see the talkative fellow who is conversing with me.'

135. The lid was raised from Balor's eye. Then Lug cast a sling stone at him which carried the eye through his head, and it was his own host that looked at it. He fell on top of the Fomorian host so that twenty-seven of them died under his side; and the crown of his head struck against the breast of Indech mac De Domnann so that a gush of blood spouted over his lips.

136. 'Let Loch Lethglas ('Halfgreen'), my poet, be summoned to me,' said Indech. (He was half green from the ground to the crown of his head.) He came to him. 'Find out for me,' said Indech, 'who hurled this cast at me.'

    Then Loch Lethglas said, 'Declare, who is the man . . .?'

    Then Lug said these words in answer to him, 'A man cast who does not fear you . . .'

137. Then the Morrigan the daughter of Ernmas came, and she was strengthening the Tuatha De to fight the battle resolutely and fiercely. She then chanted the following poem, 'Kings arise to the battle . . .'

138. Immediately afterwards the battle broke, and the Fomoire were driven to the sea. The champion Ogma

son of Elatha and Indech mac De Domnann fell
together in single combat.

In Section 133 Nuadu finally meets his death; we can infer
because the battle continues and does not automatically
come to an end at this point that he is no longer king, as
has already been commented upon. Nuadu clearly could
not handle the extreme powers being invoked during this
magical battle. This is the same scenario, but on a higher
level, that he encountered during the first battle of
Moytura, in which he likewise suffered defeat, losing his
arm. This time his defeat is greater in that he loses his life,
but he will, of course, carry on into the life of the
Otherworld.

Nuadu can in a sense be regarded as a 'warning' type of
character. Despite his position as king of the mighty
Tuatha De Danann, and despite his grand title of 'Master
of the Elements', he still suffers physical injury and now
defeat and the loss of his life. When he first appeared in
the legend he could be regarded as the ideal to which we
should all be striving, but, through no fault of his own, he
is later shown to be a failure. The warning here is not to
become too confident in your own abilities until they have
been fully tested, and to remember the inescapable fact
that perhaps your abilities are just not good enough to
cope with all situations successfully, so that consequently
sooner or later you will be defeated.

This may seem a bit harsh or pessimistic, but it is
nevertheless a fact of life on all levels and in both worlds,
and one which must be seen and recognized. Nobody in
his or her right mind expects to master everything in this
world or to be constantly successful in each and every
venture he or she turns a hand to. Why then should it be
any different for trainee magicians, who, after all, are
working with forces and beings far more powerful than
those with whom the majority of people in this world
work? The trials and tribulations of learning the new skill
of magic are just as hard and as many as those met with
in learning the techniques of any other skill. The big
difference is the results of any failure.

Section 133 contains a lengthy dialogue between Lug
and Balor; unfortunately this is one of those passages

which it is impossible for us to translate satisfactorily. As before, however, this is not of great importance for a clear understanding of the meaning behind the text, and in no way detracts from our comprehension of the legend.

Balor's magical and destructive eye is a motif which arises in many world mythologies, as is the description of its requiring several men just to physically open it. Also in common with other world mythologies, the destruction of such a malefic creature is invariably accomplished by the destruction of its evil eye. There is almost a shade of the 'good versus evil' type of morality evinced by this section, in that it is implied that to be bad simply for the sake of it will inevitably result in one's destruction at the hands of the forces for good. This, however, is a gross over-simplification of things, and it must be kept in mind that the ancient Irish Celts had no such concepts as good or evil, at least not in a moral sense. It should be noted here that Balor acquired his evil eye quite by accident, the implication being that he was as much a victim of it as were those unfortunate enough to gaze upon it.

This section lets us know that the Fomoire in common with the Tuatha De Danann had practising druids among them, although they seem to use their magical and herbal skills for destructive purposes, and in a very careless manner. The implication of this is of course that they are an inferior type of druid, and that the Fomoire generally are likewise rather inferior and destructive. Thus we have a further warning not to meddle with powerful Otherworld inhabitants should they be encountered during Otherworld journeys.

Lug is of course Balor's grandson, and the manner of Balor's death fulfils a prophesy given in some other versions of this tale, that he would die by his own grandson's hands. The number of his fellow Fomoire killed by him during his death throes, twenty-seven, is symbolic, representing a great destruction on all three levels. The significance of his blood spouting over Indech's lips is that Indech now takes on the aspect of Balor, the great champion of the Fomoire, as well as maintaining his own role of king of the Fomoire. This is echoed in Section 136, where we read that the first thing Indech does after this incident is to carry on the questioning that Balor began immediately prior to his death. It should also be noted that Balor and Indech seem to be interchangeable throughout the text, this is because they are complementary halves of each other, just as Lug and Bres are.

Indech is associated with blood. This was first hinted at in Section 85 when the Morrigan said she would 'take from him [Indech] the blood of his heart', and the text goes on to add, 'she gave two handfuls of that blood to the host'. Now here in section 135 Indech is given a bizarre sort of baptism in Balor's blood, significantly across the lips – the entrance to the mouth and therefore the passage of the voice and the breath, symbolically the soul of the person. There is obviously some magical connection here between Indech mac De Domnann and blood, but I would warn readers against trying to decipher what this connection is or to what purpose it could be put. Indech, being of the Fomoire, is not an Otherworld contact to be fostered.

Section 136 is another containing a very lengthy, untranslatable dialogue, this time between Lug and the Fomorian poet Loch Lethglas. His name, 'Half-green' is interesting in that it implies a close link with the Green World, the world of nature on the physical level, which presumably means that he was half-Fomoire, i.e. half of the Otherworld and half of this world. This, like the description of the Fomorian druids in Section 133, implies that he was a poet of lesser status than a poet of the Tuatha De Danann would be. This is probably further amplified in the untranslatable dialogue between Loch and Lug, although we cannot be sure of that. If he were a poet of the same ability as a poet of the Tuatha De Danann, he would have been able to destroy Lug with his poetic utterances and would not have entered into a one-to-one dialogue with him. This in itself is sufficient to indicate his inferior status.

Section 137 once more contains dialogue that we cannot understand, uttered this time by the Morrigan. From the opening of this section it is clear that what she says is a poetic encouragement to the men of Ireland and the warriors of the Tuatha De Danann to fight all the more valiantly, and this is the common theme of most of the untranslatable passages so far. We clearly do not need to understand these words of encouragement, for we are no longer a race or society based upon personal warrior skills; these sections are therefore, at least as far as their literal meanings go, obsolete. Judging by the amount and frequency of war continually being acted out somewhere on the planet this may not seem to be the case, but of course there is no comparison between most modern warfare and the highly skilled and individual abilities of an ancient Celtic warrior who had to rely totally on his own physical, mental and spiritual strength.

Sections 139 - 148

Sections 139 to 148 continue the description of who did what in battle, and they also return to a more magical style and reintroduce an element of ritual. Information of a generally magical nature can once again be found, as opposed to the purely warrior-related preceding sections.

139. Loch Lethglas asked Lug for quarter. 'Grant me three requests', said Lug.
140. 'You will have them', said Loch, 'I will remove the need to guard against the Fomoire from Ireland forever; and whatever judgement your tongue will deliver in any difficult case, it will resolve the matter until the end of life.'
141. So Loch was spared. Then he chanted 'The Decree of Fastening' to the Gaels . . .
142. Then Loch said that he would give names to Lug's nine chariots because he had been spared. So Lug said that he should name them. Loch answered and said, 'Luachta, Anagat, Achad, Feochair, Fer, Golla, Fosad, Craeb, Carpat.'
143. 'A question then: what are the names of the charioteers who were in them?'
    'Medol, Medon, Moth, Mothach, Foimtinne, Tenda, Tres, Morb.'
144. 'What are the names of the goads which were in their hands?'
    'Fes, Res, Roches, Anagar, Ilach, Canna, Riadha, Buaid.'

145. 'What are the names of the horses?'

    'Can, Doriadha, Romuir, Laisad, Fer Forsaid, Sroban, Airchedal, Ruagar, Ilann, Allriadha, Rocedal.'

146. 'A question: what is the number of the slain?' Lug said to Loch.

    'I do not know the number of peasants and rabble. As to the number of Fomorian lords and nobles and champions and over-kings, I do know: 3 + 3 x 20 + 50 x 100 men + 20 x 100 + 3 x 50 + 9 x 5 + 4 x 20 x 1000 + 8 + 8 x 20 + 7 + 4 x 20 + 6 + 4 x 20 + 5 + 8 x 20 + 2 + 40, including the grandson of Net with 90 men. That is the number of the slain of the Fomorian over-kings and high nobles who fell in the battle.

147. 'But regarding the number of peasants and common people and rabble and people of every art who came in company with the great host – for every warrior and every high noble and every over-king of the Fomoire came to the battle with his personal followers, so that all fell there, both their free men and their unfree servants – I count only a few of the over-kings' servants. This then is the number of those I counted as I watched: 7 + 7 x 20 x 20 x 100 x 100 + 90 including Sab Uanchennach son of Coirpre Colc, the son of a servant of Indech mac De Domnann (that is, the son of a servant of the Fomorian king.)

148. 'As for the men who fought in pairs and the spearmen, warriors who did not reach the heart of the battle who also fell there – until the stars of heaven can be counted, and the sands of the sea, and flakes of snow, and dew on a lawn, and hailstones, and grass beneath the feet of horses, and the horses of the son of Lir in a sea storm – they will not be counted at all.'

The power of Loch Lethglas, the Fomorian poet, is seen in Section 140, where he decrees that Ireland will be safe from further Fomorian invasions forever and that Lug will always be a giver of wise judgement. Lug's acceptance of his word on this matter, when no other sureties are given, demonstrates the great importance placed upon the keeping of one's word as a matter of honour by the Celts, and is also indicative of a certain amount of mercy on Lug's part, as he could quite easily kill Loch and the host of the Fomoire which remain but instead gives quarter when it is requested.

When this is agreed Loch 'seals' the agreement by a magical incantation, whose title, 'The Decree of Fastening', implies that it cannot be undone. Note the recurrence of threes in these sections, which as always throughout this legend lets us know that this particular part of the narrative deals with magical matters.

We know that the chariot was a very important battle weapon, and status symbol, to the Celts, and the introduction of chariots at this stage reflects this and also imbues them with a magical quality. As before, we do not know the meanings of all of the names given in Sections 142 to 145, but the fact that a set of four things (chariot, charioteer, goad and horse) is mentioned as opposed to the more common three, and the fact that although nine chariots were named initially only eight charioteers with eight goads to drive them and eleven horses to pull them are identified here, serve to indicate that either there has been quite a bit of corruption of the original text at this point or we are dealing with some type of magic which has lost its contemporary relevance and meaning completely. Whatever the answer, this curious part of the legend, along with the incomprehensible numerical formulae of the next two sections, must have meant something to the warrior-class and their various poets and druids at one time, but remain nothing more than frustratingly obscure and puzzling passages to us, the true and full meanings of which we shall probably never know.

It is not clear from the text why Lug asks Loch to name his chariots and charioteers, and their goads and horses. Presumably they already had names, and therefore Lug's questioning would appear to be no more than a test of Loch's psychic abilities, i.e. would he be able to determine each of their names by magical means alone? If this is the purpose behind this questioning then we can assume that Loch passes with flying colours. If, on the other hand, Lug is actually asking Loch to give all of these things new names, then this too would make sense from a magical point of view, as the giving and taking of names to signify new stages in the Great Magical Work is still a common event within modern-day magical groups.

Sections 149 - 161

The motif of the capture, questioning and subsequent release of Loch Lethglas is repeated in Sections 149 to 161, where the main character is now Bres:

149. Immediately afterward they found an opportunity to kill Bres mac Elathan. He said, 'It is better to spare me than to kill me.'

150. 'What then will follow from that?' said Lug.
    'The cows of Ireland will always be in milk,' said Bres, 'if I am spared.'
    'I will tell that to our wise men,' said Lug.

151. So Lug went to Maeltne Morbrethach and said to him, 'Shall Bres be spared for giving constant milk to the cows of Ireland?'

152. 'He shall not be spared,' said Maeltne, 'He has no power over their age or their calving, even if he controls their milk as long as they are alive.'

153. Lug said to Bres, 'That does not save you; you have no power over their age or their calving, even if you control their milk.'

154. Bres said, 'Maeltne has given bitter arms!'

155. 'Is there anything else which will save you, Bres?' said Lug.
    'There is indeed. Tell your lawyer they will reap a harvest every quarter in return for sparing me.'

156. Lug said to Maeltne, 'Shall Bres be spared for giving the men of Ireland a harvest of grain every quarter?'

157. 'This has suited us,' said Maeltne. 'Spring for plowing and sowing, and the beginning of summer for maturing the strength of the grain, and the beginning of autumn for the full ripeness of the grain, and for reaping it. Winter for consuming it.'

158. 'That does not save you,' said Lug to Bres.
    'Maeltne has given bitter alarms,' said he.

159. 'Less rescues you,' said Lug.
    'What?' asked Bres.

160. 'How shall the men of Ireland plow? How shall they

sow? How shall they reap? If you make known these things, you will be saved.'

'Say to them, on Tuesday their plowing; on Tuesday their sowing seed in the field; on Tuesday their reaping.'

161. So through that device Bres was released.

A couple of curious points crop up in these sections. First, Lug was told in the last block of text (Section 140) that he would always give wise judgement from then on, yet here he has to refer to the lawyer Maeltne Morbrethach for counsel about Bres's bargaining pleas; second, after Bres tries twice to win his life by offering something he hopes Lug will want, but subsequently rejects, it is Lug himself who in the third instance tells Bres what it is the men of Ireland need in order for his life to be spared.

It is interesting to note that after all the high magic that has been taking place, with all sorts of powerful feats being performed on both sides, everything is brought back to earth, literally, now the battle is over. Bres first claims to have power over the cattle, then over the growing seasons, and finally, after some prompting from Lug, he gives away a practical agricultural technique. All of this serves to show Bres's close links with the earth and, remembering he is Lug's complementary half, he now seems to have taken on the role of the redeemed god who fell from grace but who, thanks to the intervention of other forces and aspects of himself, has found his proper niche and has been installed in his rightful place to the benefit of all.

The significance or importance of Tuesday is totally lost to us; no doubt it originally possessed a meaning and symbolism much deeper than just representing the best day of the week for working the land. As with the questions and answers put to Loch in the previous sections, Bres's answers may actually be stating simply what the men of Ireland already practised, as the text does not say outright nor imply that Bres's answer regarding Tuesdays was anything new. Perhaps like Loch Bres was being tested on his knowledge of how things actually were rather than how they should be. We cannot be sure of the significance of these curious sections. They are clearly connected with agriculture, however, and perhaps readers interested in such matters, or already practising such things, may find it fruitful (literally!) to study these sections more deeply and try to perceive the occult information being given out in relation to agriculture.

Practical Work: Exercise 13

Tara

This exercise is an extension of the previous one, and demonstrates the way in which the simple basic ritual of drawing the circle and opening the quarters can be built upon to produce quite elaborate rituals.

Start in exactly the same way as described in Exercise 12 (page 215), but add the following: at the stage where you take each Weapon to its appropriate quarter, invoke the assistance of each of the Four Teachers of the Tuatha De Danann, with Morfesa for the north, Uiscias in the east, Esras in the south and Semias in the west. They should be visualized in exactly the same way as when you first encountered them during the first few exercises of the Practical Work. They should also be visualized with their backs to you, i.e. facing out from the circle, as they function as guardians keeping watch on anything that may approach your working area.

At the point where you are lighting each of the candles of the quarters you should now add, again in your own words, an invocation to the Elemental Power of that quarter, asking it to come and assist you in your work. This can be helped by visualizing, for Earth, tremendous movement, such as a powerful earthquake moving towards you and taking up the entire space of the northern quarter; Fire in the South can be seen as the great fiery furnace of volcanic eruptions spewing mighty mighty into the southern quarter; Air can be visualized in the east as terrific hurricanes blowing fiercely until their forceful buffeting and billowing fills that quarter; and Water can be seen as monumental, crashing waves cascading in to fill up the western quarter.

Once you have completed all this, go as before to the centre of the circle and contemplate its meaning and significance. You should now also undertake an Inner Journey to Tara, and ask admittance of the doorkeepers. The symbolism and meaning behind all this has been fully discussed in the earlier text, but the point behind this particular Inner Journey is to make you consider very seriously whether you are now ready to enter into Tara. You will have to answer all the doorkeeper's questions, just as Samildanach did – and remember this is symbolic of physical-level testing, so you must expect a certain amount of turbulence in your day-to-day life following this exercise.

Should you find yourself within Tara you will then be tested on the other levels as well, and this likewise will have manifestations on the mental and spiritual levels for several days afterwards.

Clearly this is not an Inner Journey to be undertaken lightly, and if you feel that you are not ready at this stage for such a confrontation and testing then do not attempt it. There is never any rush in this work, and it is a foolish person who thinks he or she can bend the events and beings of the Otherworld to suit his or her own desires.

These exercises can and should be repeated over and over again if any real benefit is to be gained from them, so if at first you are not prepared to carry out this particular Inner Journey, then that very realization is in itself a sign of progress. You are becoming aware of your own limitations.

Whether you decide to take this Journey or not you must still close down as described in the previous exercise. Remember to thank the Four Teachers for their guardianship and to thank the Powers of the Four Elements. All of these should be asked to return to their rightful place until they are needed again.

This stage of your Practical Work should start to make itself felt in your ordinary day-to-day life, and therefore any events, thoughts, apparent coincidences, etc. that may occur and seem important although you may not necessarily know why should be duly noted in your Magical Diary. As time goes by and as you progress you may well detect certain patterns, or consistencies (which will not necessarily always be pleasant!) developing that may hold something of personal importance. Use your intuition here. Do not fall into the trap of attributing anything and everything to your Magical Working, for this will definitely not be the case, but should something feel important then take note of it and watch for future developments.

Chapter 15
Sections 162 - 167

The final sections of the legend of *The Battle of Moytura* round everything off and leave us with a world much as we now know it, but also offer grim warnings and prophesies from the Morrigan.

162. Now in that battle Ogma the champion found Orna, the sword of Tethra, king of the Fomoire. Ogma unsheathed the sword and cleaned it. Then the sword told what had been done by it, because it was the habit of swords at that time to recount the deeds that had been done by them whenever they were unsheathed. And for that reason swords are entitled to the tribute of cleaning after they have been unsheathed. Moreover spells have been kept in swords from that time on. Now the reason why demons used to speak from weapons then is that weapons used to be worshipped by men and were among the sureties of that time. Loch Lethglas chanted the following poem about that sword . . .

163. Then Lug and the Dagda and Ogma went after the Fomoire, because they had taken the Dagda's harper, Uaithne. Eventually they reached the banqueting hall where Bres mac Elathan and Elatha mac Delbaith were. There was the harp on the wall. That is the harp in which the Dagda had bound the melodies so that they did not make a sound until he summoned them, saying,

'Come Daur Da Blao,

Come Coir Cetharchair,
Come summer, come winter,
Moutho of harps and bags and pipes!'

(Now that harp had two names, Daur Da Blao and
Coir Cetharchair.)

164. Then the harp came away from the wall, and it killed
nine men and came to the Dagda; and he played for
them the three things by which a harper is known;
sleep music, joyful music and sorrowful music. He
played sorrowful music for them so that their tearful
women wept. He played joyful music for them so that
their women and boys laughed. He played sleep
music for them so that the hosts slept. So the three
of them escaped from them unharmed – although
they wanted to kill them.

165. The Dagda brought with him the cattle taken by the
Fomoire through the lowing of the heifer which had
been given him for his work; because when she called
her calf, all the cattle of Ireland which the Fomoire
had taken as their tribute began to graze.

166. Then after the battle was won and the slaughter had
been cleaned away, the Morrigan, the daughter of
Ernmas, proceeded to announce the battle and the
great victory which had occurred there to the royal
heights of Ireland and to its sid-hosts, to its chief
waters and to its river mouths. And that is the reason
Badb still relates great deeds. 'Have you any news?'
everyone asked her then.

'Peace up to heaven.
Heaven down to earth.
Earth beneath heaven,
Strength in each,
A cup very full,
Full of honey;
Mead in abundance.
Summer in winter . . .
Peace up to heaven . . .'

167. She also prophesied the end of the world, foretelling
every evil that would occur then, and every disease

and every vengeance; and she chanted the following poem:

I shall not see a world
Which will be dear to me;
Summer without blossoms,
Cattle will be without milk,
Women without modesty,
Men without valour.
Conquests without a king . . .
Woods without mast.
Sea without produce . . .
False judgements of old men.
False precedents of lawyers,
Every man a betrayer.
Every son a reaver.
The son will go to the bed of his father,
The father will go to the bed of his son.
Each his brother's brother-in-law.
He will not seek any woman outside his house . . .
An evil time,
Son will deceive his father,
Daughter will deceive . . .'

Section 162

This final block of the narrative contains information that is a little bit more useful than that of the immediately preceding sections. Section 162 gives a description of the potency and importance of swords, especially when used not only as battle weapons but as magical tools as well. It also stresses the gravity of treating such tools with respect, and this still applies today, not just to magical swords but to all the other magical weapons, tools, paraphernalia, and indeed, words, phrases and movements employed by a modern-day magical group.

This respect is something that every novice magician should keep in mind, and apart from the obvious displays of respect such as handling things carefully and keeping them clean and in good repair it should also be manifest in the way that certain things are talked about, or not talked about, as the case may be. This respectful attitude is as much a part of the magician's training as learning the correct words, movements, states of mind, etc., which most people initially think of when magical training is discussed. Respect is also one of the reasons behind the so-called occult secrecy most groups and individuals active in this Great Work maintain. The four maxims of any magician should be To Know, To Will, To Dare and *To Keep Silent.*

Sections 163 – 167

From Section 163 onwards we seem to have stepped back in time to a period when the battle was still going on, or at least was in its final stages, with the Fomoire in retreat. According to this section, among the company who went in pursuit of the Dagda's harp was the champion Ogma, yet in Section 138 (page 223) we were told that Ogma fell during the battle. This whole incident of the recovery of the stolen harp is an odd one, but its overall feel is that it is of importance and hidden meaning. By placing it at such an important point in the legend it was obviously intended to be noted carefully by those studying the narrative.

This part of the legend does, however, appear to contradict itself in a couple of places. In the first sentence the implication is that Lug, the Dagda and Ogma have gone to the Fomoire to rescue a person, namely Uaithne, the Dagda's harper. Thereafter however he is not mentioned again, and it is in fact the harp itself that is rescued. Also, why is Uaithne called 'the Dagda's harper', when we are later told that only the Dagda himself can summon the melodies magically bound within his harp, and in Section 164, once he has it in his grasp, it is the Dagda who plays it and not Uaithne?

The names of the harp, Daur Da Blao and Coir Cetharchair, mean 'Oak of Two Meadows' and 'Just [or Fitting] Square [or Rectangle]'. Both names are clearly intended to be magical, with their obvious dual and Polar attributes. It was also noted in our discussion of Section 93 (page 189) that the Dagda is associated with the oak tree, and this is emphasized again in this section by the

first name given to his harp. The playing of the three
strains of music has already been introduced with
Samildanach in Section 73 (page 169), and this coupled
with the magical powers of the harp all adds up to make
this part of the narrative, which in the sections
immediately previous has been very down-to-earth and
basic, once more take on the more magical and mysterious
air of the earlier text. This may be deliberate in that we
are coming to the close of the legend and perhaps the
composers of this masterly piece did not wish it to finish
with a rather mundane and predictable incident, such as
the defeating of the Fomoire in battle, but instead
wished to leave their audience with an aura of mystery
and Otherworldliness surrounding the tale they had just
been given.

The reason for the Dagda's being advised to ask for
a cow as payment for his labour during Bres's corrupt
reign (Section 32, page 107) now also becomes clear,
as this cow has the power to control all the other cattle of
Ireland. Cattle were currency to the Irish Celts, and
very much status symbols and signs of wealth
and prosperity. On a more magical level, a cow was a
frequent symbol of the Goddess of Sovereignty, the
fertility of the land itself.

The last two sections continue the magical theme but
also add in dire warnings of what is going to befall the
world in ages to come. This of course is not unique
to the Irish system, and is more or less the stock in
trade of mythology and eschatology throughout the
world; here it also serves to remind us very strongly that
the events of the legend we have just read, or listened to,
have culminated in the time and place we find ourselves
in at this moment, and that unless we adopt the
instructions given throughout the text of the legend,
these dreadful circumstances are what we can expect
and are no more than we deserve. The way to stop
them happening and put to right the wrongs that
already exist within our world, lies within us all. Each
of us has an individual responsibility to face up to and
deal with these things. You have been given the
information necessary to find out how to do this - now go
and do it!

Practical Work: Exercise 14

Sovereignty

The final exercise in this series follows on from the previous two. You should carry out everything as described in Exercise 13, but here instead of making an Inner Journey to Tara you should now attempt a link with the Sovereignty of the Land, the Goddess of Earth. This Journey represents the culmination, at least at this level, of your Magical Workings.

Some readers may find the symbolism in this Inner Journey a bit odd or difficult to cope with due to its apparent sexual orientation, but you must remember that at this level of working there is no Polarity, no differentiation of the physical sexes, and therefore you are neither female nor male: You just are. It is necessary, however, to represent what is going on in terms that your consciousness can picture and understand; hence the need to employ such imagery in order for the 'higher' meaning to come across and make the very deep and important changes necessary within your spiritual aspects. In Irish Celtic Tradition Sovereignty was always portrayed as female, and for consistency's sake we have adopted that description here. Should any reader feel more comfortable with the image of a man then that visualization will occur naturally for him or her anyway. Better still, if you can set aside your self-identification with a physical sex for the brief duration of this Inner Journey it will wield far more power than if you let mundane thoughts and emotions block its higher flow.

Once you have opened the circle, invoked the guardians and the Elements, etc., you should spend a brief moment contemplating the significance of the Inner Journey you are about to undertake, i.e. the mating with the Sovereignty of the Earth itself. When you are ready, commence your Inner Journey in the usual way by closing down your outer senses and thoughts and opening up your more potent Inner ones.

The scene before you is a very misty woodland at dawn. There is some thin grass about your feet and the mist swirls and floats around the trunks of great trees, whose tops disappear into the mist. It is very still and you feel very fresh and alert in the crisp, cool air. There is a little skiff of snow on the ground.

Presently you realize that someone or something is coming towards you through the mist. You hear twigs breaking and the general sound of movement getting louder and louder as you stand with bated breath waiting to see the source of this interruption. Suddenly a bulky shape looms up before you out of the mist. You see that it is a black-and-white spotted cow with great horns and a long, shaggy tail. It is obviously a cow, but somehow it looks different from the domestic beasts we are familiar with nowadays. It seems bigger, coarser and more muscular. It stares at you for a moment with its big, soft brown eyes, then turns and starts to shamble off into the mist again. You follow instinctively.

The cow never looks back as you walk along behind it through the thick forest and mist. As you walk you feel your consciousness moving to a higher level and your general sense of excitement and awareness increases. The trees start to thin out, as does the mist, until you come to a deep, black river along the bank of which the cow turns and walks. The sun is just beginning to rise, the mist is lifting, and you can see that this river seems to meander for miles through rolling countryside of green, uncultivated fields dotted here and there with patches of melting snow. Something ahead on a slight hillock catches your eye, but you cannot make out exactly what it is. Something white and very large.

As you get nearer you can see over the cow's shoulders that there are several large standing stones in the field ahead, and that atop the little hill is a massive earth mound which has walls some ten or eleven feet high and covered in pure white quartz. As you draw near this huge circular mound with its shining white walls you see a massive stone lying in front of and set slightly into the quartz walls, in what looks like the entrance to this great earth mound. This stone is carved with great triple spirals and diamond shapes, and you walk round it, still following the cow, and enter the tall, narrow opening of a tunnel, which leads into the very heart of the massive earth mound.

Inside it is very dark and you cannot see anything at all. You must feel your way forward slowly in the blackness as the ground beneath your feet rises gently upwards. You can hear the soft padding of the cow's hoofs as it slowly ambles up this stone-lined tunnel towards the mound's centre. After a moment two things occur to you: first, that the distance you have already walked along this tunnel would seem to be much greater than the outside size of the whole mound would suggest possible, and second, that the sound of the cow walking in the blackness in front of you has changed. Its breathing has become quieter and slightly faster, and the sound of its horny hoofs on the stone below your feet has changed to a very gentle padding, just like the sound your own feet are making.

Suddenly the stone walls on either side of you, which you have been drawing your hands along to guide you, disappear, and you can sense that you have just stepped into a much wider and higher area. The sound of movement ahead of you has also stopped, and all that your senses can pick out in the utter blackness is a soft breathing, a human breathing, slightly in front of you. Instinctively you turn and look to the tunnel you have just walked along. You cannot see it, but none the less you stand in the silence and blackness and look back towards it.

In the silence and darkness there is a steady warmth which gives you a feeling of great comfort. You feel alienated but at the same time warm and safe, as if inside there is something which is itself protecting you. Time has stopped. You feel as if you have been in the darkness for as long as you can remember. You have difficulty recalling just who you are and why you are here. It is as if you are actually thinking about an old acquaintance rather than yourself.

You start to tense up slightly as you realize that you can perceive a faint glow coming from the mouth of the tunnel, a very long way off. This glow gets steadily stronger and brighter and starts to take on the form of a shaft of brilliant white light slowly creeping along the floor of the tunnel towards you. As it comes nearer you step aside to let it pass, and you watch fascinated as it starts to illuminate the great cross-shaped chamber in which you stand. The light moves up the wall of the back of the chamber and, as it does so, it illuminates the body of a perfectly formed, naked female figure. The cow which had lead you into this place is nowhere to be seen, and instead you are gazing upon the shape of a beautiful naked woman who seems to be absorbing and radiating the sunlight that is piercing its way into the chamber.

You cannot look away from this image of perfect beauty and serenity, and you feel yourself almost involuntarily shuffling towards her across the earthen floor of this stone chamber. The light has continued moving and is now shining on the triple spiral symbol carved into the stone on the back wall of the recess in which the woman stands. She herself still seems to be radiating light from her own body. Just as you get next to her the light from the tunnel behind you fades and disappears as suddenly as it appeared, and you are once again plunged into utter darkness. The woman's body has stopped radiating light, but now you feel her warm, soft skin against your hands as you caress her beautiful form in the blackness.

At this point there are several things that can happen, and it is impossible for me to tell you exactly what is the 'correct' experience for you at this vitally important stage. You must trust your own intuitions and abilities and take things exactly as they come. You must realize that this figure of Sovereignty has as much free-will as you have, and she may thus choose to reject you if you are not yet fully ready for such an important mating.

You must also learn not to consciously or unconsciously place value judgements, or moral judgements, on what you are doing, as you are in a place and a state of being where such considerations are totally irrelevant and, in a sense, sacrilegious. Whatever happens for you at this point, assuming you have entered into this Working in the correct frame of mind and with the correct intentions, will be what is meant to happen, and you will know instinctively that it is right.

When the time feels right you must leave this place and return to the world outside along the black, stone tunnel. The woman does not come with you, and you make your way along the downward sloping tunnel alone. As you do so you realize that you have been changed quite dramatically, and that the way you see and understand the world will never be the same again after this. Eventually you make out bright light ahead, and soon you step out from behind the large carved stone at the entrance to this important place into the bright but muted sunshine of a winter's morning. There is a large black-and-white spotted cow grazing contentedly a short way ahead of you.

There is no need to make your way back to the woodlands where this Inner Journey commenced. Close down your Inner senses and prepare to return to normal day-to-day consciousness within your body within the circle. Once you are fully physically aware you should thank and dismiss the guardians and Elements and close down the circle as described in the previous Exercises. Write up your Magical Diary and close down your psychic centres and senses with food and a hot drink.

Afterword

This book has hardly even scratched the surface of the Irish Celtic Magical Tradition, but it should have given the serious reader enough information and guidance to encourage further study of the system, and if the Practical Work has been followed with the correct intentions and in the manner described you should now be capable of furthering your own studies either through direct personal experience or by following the guidance given in some of the more advanced books on the subject as listed in the Bibliography.

To some readers parts of *The Battle of Moytura* may have appeared crude or violent; to others it may have seemed in places disturbing or cruel. The Irish Celtic Magical Tradition is not suited to everyone, and if after reading this book you feel it is not the system for you, then that at least is a positive step in itself, for you have learned about yourself.

For those of you who feel you have gained from this study of the system and would like to know more, then you can do no better than to read further Irish legends, particularly in the accurate translations provided by the Irish Texts Society, and applying the interpretive principles set out in this book to your reading of them. You will begin to see that each one has its own special and individual instruction and function, and that a vast body of lore and knowledge can be built up from this. However, at the end of the day always remember that nobody can, or will, learn for you. The onus is on you to develop and improve yourself without passing the responsibility on to others - so don't just sit there, go out and do it!

Bibliography

The Celts

Anderson, Joseph, *Scotland in Pagan Times*, 2 vols, Edinburgh: Douglas, 1886.

Chadwick, Nora, *The Celts*, London: Pelican, 1971.

Cunliffe, B., *The Celtic World*, London: The Bodley Head, 1979.

Delaney, Frank, *The Celts*, London: BBC Publications, 1986.

Forman, W., and Kruta, V., *The Celts of the West*, London: Orbis, 1985.

Harbison, Peter, *Pre-Christian Ireland*, London: Thames & Hudson, 1988.

Herm, Gerhardt, *The Celts*, London: Weidenfeld & Nicolson, 1976.

Hubert, H. *The Rise of the Celts*, London: Constable, 1987.

— *The Greatness and Decline of the Celts*, London: Constable, 1987.

Joyce, P. W., *A Social History of Ancient Ireland*, Harlow: Longmans, 1903.

Keating, Geoffrey, *The History of Ireland*, 4 vols., London: Irish Texts Society, 1902, 1908, 1914.

Lebor Na Cert, London: Irish Texts Society, 1962.

MacKenzie, Donald, *Scotland the Ancient Kingdom*, Glasgow: Blackie, 1930.

MacKenzie, W. C., *The Races of Ireland and Scotland*, Paisley: Gardner, 1915.

Markale, Jean, *Women of the Celts*, Paris: Inner Traditions, 1986.

Matthews, John, *Boudicca*, Dorset. Firebird Books, 1988.

Newark, Tim, *Celtic Warriors*, London: Blandford, 1986.

— *Women Warlords*, London: Blandford, 1989.

Piggot, Stuart, *The Druids*, London: Thames & Hudson, 1985.

Powell, T.G.E., *The Celts*, London: Thames & Hudson, 1983.

Ross, Anne, *Pagan Celtic Britain*, London: RKP, 1967.

Rutherford, Ward, *The Druids*, Wellingborough: The Aquarian Press, 1983.

Spence, Lewis, *History and Origins of Druidism*, Wellingborough: The Aquarian Press, 1971.

Celtic Mythology

Bellingham, David, *An Introduction to Celtic Mythology*, London: The Apple Press, 1990.

Berresford Ellis, Peter, *A Dictionary of Irish Mythology*, London: Constable, 1987.

Book of Leinster Tain, London: Irish Texts Society, 1969.

Buile Suibhne Geilt, London: Irish Texts Society, 1913.

Caldecott, Moyra, *Women In Celtic Myth*, London: Arrow Books, 1988.

Cath Maige Mucraime, London: Irish Texts Society, 1975.

Cath Maige Tuired, London: Irish Texts Society, 1983.

Cross, T.P., and Slover, C.H., *Ancient Irish Tales*, Dublin: Figgis, 1936.

Delaney, Frank, *Legends of the Celts*, London: Hodder & Stoughton, 1989.

Dillon, Miles, *Cycles of the Irish Kings*, Oxford: Oxford University Press, 1946.

— *Irish Sagas*, Dublin: Mercier, 1985.

Dillon, M., and Chadwick, N., *The Celtic Realms*, London: Weidenfeld & Nicolson, 1967.

Duanaire Finn, 3 vols., London: Irish Texts Society, 1908, 1933, 1954.

Fled Bricrend, London: Irish Texts Society, 1899.

Gantz, J., *Early Irish Myths and Sagas*, London: Penguin, 1981.

Gregory, Lady Augusta, *Cuchulainn of Muirthemne*, Gerrards Cross: Smythe, 1984.

— *Gods and Fighting Men*, Gerrards Cross: Smythe, 1979.

Hull, E., *The Cuchulainn Saga*, London: George G. Harrap & Co., 1911.

Jackson, Kenneth, *A Celtic Miscellany*, London: RKP, 1951.

Joyce, P.W., *Old Celtic Romances*, London: Kegan Paul, 1879.

Kinsella, Thomas, *The Tain*, Oxford: Oxford University Press, 1986.

Lebor Gabala Erenn, 5 vols., London: Irish Texts Society, 1938 - 56.

MacCana, P., *Celtic Mythology*, London: Hamlyn, 1975.

— *The Learned Tales of Medieval Ireland*, Dublin: Institute for Advanced Studies, 1980.

Matthews, John, *Fionn MacCumhaill*, Dorset: Firebird Books, 1988.

Matthews, John, and Matthews, Caitlín, *The Aquarian Guide to British and Irish Mythology*, Wellingborough: The Aquarian Press, 1988.

Meyer, Kuno, *Death Tales of the Ulster Heroes*, Hodges, 1906.

— *The Voyage of Bran, Son of Febal*, Nutt, 1895.

Neeson, Eoin, *First Book of Irish Myths and Legends*, Dublin: Mercier, 1981.

— *Second Book of Irish Myths and Legends*, Dublin: Mercier, 1982.

O'Rahilly, T.F., *Early Irish History and Mythology*, Dublin: Institute for Advanced Studies, 1946.

Rees A., and Rees, B., *Celtic Heritage*, London: Thames & Hudson, 1974.

Rhys, J., *The Hibbert Lectures*, London: Williams & Norgate, 1888.

Rolleston, T.W., *Celtic Myths and Legends*, London: Bracken Books, 1985.

Smyth, D., *A Guide to Irish Mythology*, Dublin: Irish Academic Press, 1988.

Squire, Charles, *Celtic Myth and Legend*, Henley-on-Thames: Gresham, 1905.

Stewart, R.J., *Celtic Gods, Celtic Goddesses*, London: Blandford, 1990.

— *Cuchulainn*, Dorset: Firebird Books, 1988.

Toraidheacht Dhiarmada Agus Ghrainne, London: Irish Texts Society, 1967.

Williamson, Robin, *The Craneskin Bag*, Edinburgh: Canongate, 1989.

Young, Ella, *Celtic Wonder Tales*, Edinburgh: Floris Books, 1983.

Magic and The Western Mystery Tradition

Adler, Margaret, *Drawing Down the Moon*, Boston, Mass.: Beacon Press, 1979.

Ashcroft-Nowicki, Dolores, *First Steps in Ritual*, Wellingborough: The Aquarian Press, 1982.

— *The Shining Paths*, Wellingborough: The Aquarian Press, 1983.

Carr-Gomm, Philip, *The Elements of the Druid Tradition*, Shaftesbury: Element Books, 1991.

Green, Marian, *Magic for the Aquarian Age*, Wellingborough: The Aquarian Press, 1983.

— *Experiments in Aquarian Magic*, Wellingborough: The Aquarian Press, 1985.

— *The Elements of Natural Magic*, Shaftesbury: Element Books, 1989.

— *The Path Through the Labyrinth*, Shaftesbury: Element Books, 1985.

Hartley, Christine, *The Western Mystery Tradition*, Wellingborough: The Aquarian Press, 1968.

Hope, Murry, *Practical Celtic Magic*, Wellingborough: The Aquarian Press, 1987.

Knight, Gareth, *The Rose Cross and The Goddess*, Wellingborough: The Aquarian Press, 1985.

— *The Secret Tradition in Arthurian Legend*, Wellingborough: The Aquarian Press, 1983.

Matthews, Caitlín, *The Elements of the Celtic Tradition*, Shaftesbury: Element Books, 1989.

Matthews, Caitlín, and Matthews, John, *The Western Way*, 2 vols. Arkana, 1985.

Matthews, Caitlín, and Jones, Prudence, *Voices from the Circle*, Wellingborough: The Aquarian Press, 1989.

Matthews, John, *The Grail: Quest for Eternal Life*,

London: Thames & Hudson, 1981.
— *The Elements of the Arthurian Tradition*, Shaftesbury: Element Books, 1989.
Nichols, Ross, *The Book of Druidry*, London: The Aquarian Press, 1990.
Richardson, Alan, *Gate of Moon*, Wellingborough: The Aquarian Press, 1984.
Sharkey, John, *Celtic Mysteries*, London: Thames & Hudson, 1975.
Spence, Lewis, *Magic Arts in Celtic Britain*, London: The Aquarian Press, 1970.
Stewart, R.J., *The Underworld Initiation*, Wellingborough: The Aquarian Press, 1988.
— *Living Magical Arts*, London: Blandford, 1987.
— *Advanced Magical Arts*, Shaftesbury: Element Books, 1988.

The Celtic Soul

As an Fhearann, Edinburgh: Mainstream Publishing, 1986.
Campbell, J.F., *Popular Tales of the West Highlands*, 4 vols., Aldershot: Wildwood House, 1983.
Carmichael, Alex, *Carmina Gadelica*, 2 vols., Edinburgh: Oliver & Boyd, 1928.
Danaher, Kevin, *The Year in Ireland*, Dublin: Mercier, 1972.
Evans-Wentz, W.Y., *Fairy Faith in Celtic Countries*, Gerrards Cross: Smythe, 1977.
Greene, David, *An Anthology of Irish Literature*, 2 vols. New York: NYU Press.
Macleod, Fiona, *The Collected Works*, 7 vols. London: Heinemann, 1910.
Matthews, John, *A Celtic Reader*, London: The Aquarian Press, 1990.
Merry, Eleanor, *The Flaming Door*, Edinburgh: Floris Books, 1983.
Yeats, William Butler, *The Collected Poems*, London: Pan Books, 1990.

Discography

All recordings by the following artistes are recommended:

Black-eyed Biddy
Christy Moore
Moving Hearts
Planxty
Runrig
Sileas
Alan Stivell
Tannahill Weavers
Whistlebinkies
Robin Williamson

Robin Williamson produces excellent story tapes as well as excellent music. Write to: Robin Williamson Productions, BCM 4797, London, WC1N 3XX for a full catalogue.

Sulis Music & Tapes, BCM Box 3721, London WC1N 3XX produce many musical and magical tapes of a very high standard.

Journals and Societies

Cambridge Medieval Celtic Studies, Department of Anglo-Saxon, Norse & Celtic, 9 West Road, Cambridge, CB3 9DP.

Emania, the journal of the Navan Fort Research Group, Department of Archaeology, Queen's University, Belfast, BT7 1NN, Northern Ireland.

Irish Texts Society, c/o The Royal Bank of Scotland, 22 Whitehall, London SW1. Produce the best translations of Irish legends available, all with extensive notes and glossaries.

Order of Bards, Ovates and Druids, 260 Kew Road, Richmond, Surrey TW9 3EG.

Pagan Life, the newsletter of the Irish Pagan Movement, The Bridge House, Clonegal, Enniscorthy, Co. Wexford, Eire.

PAS Newsletter, Pictish Arts Society, School of Scottish Studies, 27 George Square, Edinburgh, EH8 9LD.

Seanchas, the journal of the Celtic Research & Folklore

Society, Isle of Arran, Scotland.

Shadow, the journal of the Traditional Cosmology Society, School of Scottish Studies, 27 George Square, Edinburgh, EH8 9LD.

Index